NONE ELSE

NONE ELSE

31 Meditations on God's
Character and Attributes

Joel R. Beeke
and
Brian Cosby

Reformation Heritage Books
Grand Rapids, Michigan

None Else
© 2020 by Joel R. Beeke and Brian Cosby

Reformation Heritage Books
3070 29th St. SE
Grand Rapids, MI 49512
616-977-0889
orders@heritagebooks.org
www.heritagebooks.org

Printed in the United States of America
21 22 23 24 25 26/10 9 8 7 6 5 4 3 2

Library of Congress Cataloging-in-Publication Data

Names: Beeke, Joel R., 1952- author. | Cosby, Brian H., author.
Title: None else : 31 meditations on God's character and attributes /
    Joel R. Beeke and Brian Cosby.
Description: Grand Rapids, Michigan : Reformation Heritage Books,
    2020. | Includes bibliographical references.
Identifiers: LCCN 2020017191 (print) | LCCN 2020017192 (ebook) |
    ISBN 9781601787996 (paperback) | ISBN 9781601788009 (epub)
Subjects: LCSH: God (Christianity)—Attributes—Meditations.
Classification: LCC BT130 .B44 2020 (print) | LCC BT130 (ebook) |
    DDC 231/.4—dc23
LC record available at https://lccn.loc.gov/2020017191
LC ebook record available at https://lccn.loc.gov/2020017192

For additional Reformed literature, request a free book list from Reformation Heritage Books at the above regular or email address.

CONTENTS

Contents

To
Laura Beeke, James Engelsma, and Isaac Epp
three God-fearing, very special in-law children,
who Mary and I love greatly in Christ Jesus.
Thanks so much for blessing our children and us
with yourself and with our precious grandchildren.

I have no greater joy than to hear [and know and see!]
that my children walk in truth (3 John 4).

—JRB

To
Charles Barrett and Nick Batzig
pastors with whom I am privileged to serve alongside
at Wayside Presbyterian Church (PCA).
Thank you for your Christlike example, friendship,
and encouragement in gospel ministry.

Therefore seeing we have this ministry,
as we have received mercy, we faint not (2 Cor. 4:1).

—BC

INTRODUCTION: 1
MEDITATING ON GOD'S CHARACTER

The purpose of this book is to guide genuine Christians, reading one chapter a day, in meditating on God's perfect character and attributes for one month so that your mind will be transformed, your affections kindled, and your faith nourished by His grace. Many competing distractions attempt to steal your time and fill your schedule so that you are tempted by sheer busyness from taking time to meditate on the triune God whom you love as a true believer.

Some of these distractions can functionally take the place of God in our lives—idols pulling our minds and affections away from the Creator and toward the creation.

But God calls us to "know that the LORD he is God; there is none else beside him" (Deut. 4:35). *None else.* Peter asked Jesus the rhetorical question, "Lord, to whom shall we go? Thou hast the words of eternal life" (John 6:68). There is no other. *None else.* But who *is* this God and how are we to "know" that He is the sovereign Lord of all?

The answer to those questions is the aim of this book.

It is our hope that you will use this guide and resource to focus your thoughts on and channel your love toward the God who is. May His perfect character instill greater desire and love for Him and may the gospel of Jesus Christ be evident as it is displayed from God's manifold attributes. Indeed, "unto him that is able to keep you from falling, and to present you faultless before the presence of his glory with exceeding joy, to the only wise God our Saviour, be glory and majesty, dominion and power, both now and ever. Amen" (Jude 24–25).

Meditating on God's Word is one of the most rewarding and faith-sustaining disciplines in the Christian life. It ushers the believer into greater communion with God and satisfies the longing soul. Meditation is a lingering over, a chewing on, and a wrestling with God's Word until—like Jacob wrestling with the angel—you are blessed by its promises and nourished by its truth.

The purpose of this book is to provide you with meditations on God's character and attributes so that you will grow in both knowledge of and love for the Rock of your salvation by the Spirit's grace. While there are many devotionals in the marketplace offering guidance into the treasures of God's Word, *None Else* specifically reflects on God's manifold perfections as a means through which He—by His Spirit—graciously transforms our minds, changes our hearts, and molds us into the image of His Son, Jesus Christ.

For each attribute, we seek to help you enter into a deeper relationship with God by organizing the material into the following sections for each attribute:

- Scripture Meditation
- Prayer
- Biblical Perspective
- Reflection Questions
- Digging Deeper

These are meant to be practical directional signs, pointing to the true and living God and His gracious work of drawing sinners into a living and active fellowship with Him.

In each meditation, the full Scripture passage is given so that you may conveniently reference the text as you go along in your study and reflection upon God's character. It is recommended, however, that you have your own copy of the Bible available to look up various passages referenced or to read the surrounding context. It is also recommended that you read through the passage slowly and intentionally, thinking about each word and the overall message. In fact, it would be best to read the passage out loud several times as you work through each day's meditation.

Praying at the start of each meditation is meant to set your mind afresh on this delight and privilege. The prayers are taken from the passage and are meant to remind you of God's absolute power, wisdom, and love, and as a true believer, of your absolute dependence upon Him as your heavenly Father. Ask God to give you a teachable and soft heart to be instructed, encouraged, challenged, and changed. Prayer is possible only through the mediation of Jesus Christ. As the writer of Hebrews exhorts: "Having therefore, brethren, boldness to enter into the holiest by the blood of Jesus, by a new and living way, which he hath consecrated for us, through the veil, that is to say, his flesh; and having an high priest over the house of God; let us draw near, with a true heart in full assurance of faith" (Heb. 10:19–22).

Furthermore, we are to pray *expectantly*, with full assurance of our position and righteous standing before God. Because our sin has been credited—*imputed*—to Christ's account and His righteousness credited to our account by faith alone, we have been declared "not guilty" before a holy and just God. This, of course, is the doctrine of justification by faith alone. We can, therefore, enter into God's presence with prayers of praise, confession, intercession, thanksgiving, and supplication.

The section titled "Biblical Perspective" simply explains some of the biblical, historical, and theological background of the attribute of God under study and guides your thoughts on the truths of that attribute. It will also seek to show how each attribute is related to the gospel of Jesus Christ.

Jesus Himself explained that all of Scripture points to Him and His life-work. While He was walking on the road to Emmaus after His resurrection, He tells His traveling companions that all of Scripture points to Him. Luke records, "And beginning at Moses and all the prophets, he expounded unto them in all the scriptures the things concerning himself" (Luke 24:27). The apostle Paul writes in 2 Corinthians 1:20 that "all the promises of God in him are yea." Indeed, the Word of God is chiefly about the *Word* of God (John 1:1), Jesus Christ.

Reflection questions are provided with each chapter to help you think through how the truth of God's character influences and directs your daily life. This is meant to be a very practical section in which probing questions are asked of your habits, thoughts, emotions, and actions. Space is also provided for you to write down your thoughts so as to remember them later or share them with others. To be sure, this will take some discipline, time, and honesty as you think through the implications of God's attributes and how Christ's strength is made perfect in your weakness (2 Cor. 12:9).

The final section in each chapter, "Digging Deeper," provides further Scripture passages, questions, thoughts, quotations, and other resources on each characteristic of God. If you find yourself especially encouraged by a certain attribute of God, then you may find this section particularly helpful.

It is important to remember that we are to *meditate* on God in His Word. The psalmist writes that the believer is blessed when "his delight is in the law of the LORD; and in his law doth he meditate day and night" (Ps. 1:2). He goes on to say that he "shall be like a tree planted by the rivers of water, that bringeth forth his fruit in his season; his leaf also shall not wither" (v. 3). In other words, by His Spirit's grace, God is in the business of planting us and growing us into trees of righteousness (Isa. 61:3) through meditation on His Word. In addition, meditation will lead to the increase of spiritual fruit—love, joy, peace, patience, kindness, goodness, faithfulness, gentleness, and self-control (Gal. 5:22–23).

In the sixteenth century, Martin Luther helped start what we now call the Protestant Reformation—a movement that eventually led to a break from the Roman Catholic Church. Luther debated many people over the nature of salvation, faith, and the authority of the church. One of those people was a man named Erasmus, who believed that humans had the moral freedom to choose God on their own. Luther responded in a letter to Erasmus by saying, "Your thoughts concerning God are too human."[1]

---

1. Martin Luther, *The Bondage of the Will* (Lafayette, Ind.: Sovereign Grace Publishers, 2001), 22.

Perhaps as you pick up this book, you find that your thoughts on God are far too human. Maybe you have succumbed, like many of us, to the temptation to believe that we are entitled to blessings from God. The truth is that nobody has arrived at a complete understanding of who God is in His fullness. Paul writes, however, that we are "stewards of the mysteries of God" (1 Cor. 4:1). We have been given the privilege of discovering, learning about, and experiencing more and more the character of God—for His glory and our joy.

We wish to thank our dear wives for their faithful support as we persevered in writing this book. Thanks also to Ian Turner for his valuable assistance and Travis Childers and Ray Lanning for their able editorial pass. May this book of meditations encourage your heart, strengthen your faith, and grow your affections for God. May you see more and more of the riches of the gospel of Jesus Christ, for "it pleased the Father that in him should all fulness dwell" (Col. 1:19). And may you find yourself in a deeper, more satisfying communion with your Savior and Lord.

THE TRUE KNOWLEDGE OF GOD

2

SCRIPTURE MEDITATION

Thus saith the LORD, Let not the wise man glory in his wisdom, neither let the mighty man glory in his might, let not the rich man glory in his riches: but let him that glorieth glory in this, that he understandeth and knoweth me, that I am the LORD which exercise lovingkindness, judgment, and righteousness, in the earth: for in these things I delight, saith the LORD.

—JEREMIAH 9:23–24[1]

PRAYER

Lord God, I thank Thee for the gift of knowing Thee. Thou art a gracious, covenant-keeping redeemer, and the worth of knowing Thee far surpasses anything else I could set my heart on. Grant me fresh views of Thy glory in Christ to awaken me from spiritual slumber. As I pursue Christ by faith, continue to renew me in knowledge after Thy image. Grant me understanding through fearing and loving Thee.

---

1. Some material from Joel R. Beeke's chapters has been adapted from Joel R. Beeke and Paul Smalley, *Reformed Systematic Theology, Volume 1: Revelation and God* (Wheaton, Ill.: Crossway, 2019).

Make my knowledge of Thee bear fruit in all that is pleasing to Thee. I pray in Jesus's name. Amen.

BIBLICAL PERSPECTIVE

Knowing God and making Him known are the heartbeat of what it means to be human. Calvin asks in his catechism, "What is the chief end of human life?" He answers, "To know God."[2] There are several reasons the knowledge of God is central and supreme for all human life.

First, knowing God is your highest *privilege*. We often think that if we achieve "wisdom," "might," or "riches," then our life has meaning and worth. But God declares that these "boasts" and privileges are not worth our esteem: "But let him that glorieth glory in this, that he understandeth and knoweth me" (Jer. 9:23–24). Many wise, mighty, and wealthy people on their deathbeds arrive at the same conclusion as the Preacher, "I have seen all the works that are done under the sun; and, behold, all is vanity and vexation of spirit" (Eccl. 1:14). Elevating other pursuits above God in our lives fills our hearts with worldliness, which diminishes our souls and makes us petty. But by learning, experiencing, and rejoicing in the knowledge of God, we receive the greatest of blessings and God receives the highest glory. We were created for the greatest of gifts: knowing God.

Second, knowing God is the heart of the *covenant* and the essence of *eternal life*. Our idolatry, sin, and false worship are linked to our ignorance of God: "They know not me, saith the LORD"; "there is no truth, nor mercy, nor knowledge of

---

2. Phillip Schaff, *Creeds of Christendom* (New York: Harper & Brothers, 1877), 1:470.

God in the land" (Jer. 9:3; Hos. 4:1). But in His grace God announces, "Behold, the days come, saith the LORD, that I will make a new covenant with the house of Israel"—which will bring the blessing of the knowledge of God: "they shall all know me, from the least of them unto the greatest of them" (Jer. 31:31–34). Such knowledge stems from the gift of a new heart—a "heart to know me, that I am the LORD: and they shall be my people, and I will be their God" (Jer. 24:7). Since knowledge of God is a gift of the "everlasting covenant" (Jer. 32:40), Jesus can then say, "and this is life eternal, that they might know thee the only true God, and Jesus Christ, whom thou hast sent" (John 17:3). Your eternal communion with God is based on the true knowledge of God.

Third, knowing God is the engine of *holiness* in our lives. When we forsake the knowledge of God, our hearts become foolish and darkened, since we "changed the truth of God into a lie, and worshipped and served the creature more than the Creator, who is blessed for ever" (Rom. 1:21–25). Ignorance of God plunges us into idolatry, which fuels injustice and immorality in our lives (1 Thess. 4:5; Hos. 4:1–2). Often, the turning point in our times of spiritual decline is a fresh view of God (see Job 42:1–6). The growth that God gives us in "grace and peace" and "all things that pertain to life and godliness" comes "through the knowledge of God, and of Jesus our Lord...of him that hath called us to glory and virtue" (2 Pet. 1:2–3). False ideas about God lead to shallow spirituality that mimics the world, but true knowledge of God—brought to us by God's "exceeding great and precious promises"—produces deep, meaningful, and Spirit-empowered godliness (2 Pet. 1:4).

Knowing God is therefore the central priority of your life. To Paul, all the honors and privileges of this world are "but dung" compared to "the excellency of the knowledge of Christ Jesus my Lord" (Phil. 3:8). How, then, do we seek the knowledge of God and "follow on to know the LORD" throughout our lives (Hos. 6:3)? The knowledge of God is fundamentally relational; we seek it by seeking *Him* in at least five ways.

First, we must be *dependent* upon and *receptive* to God. We do not *discover* the knowledge of God, but receive it. God must reveal Himself to us, on His own initiative, by His Word (Matt. 11:27). Too often we can be like some theologians who conjure deep thoughts of God that are only a product of our own imaginations. Rather, we must receive what God has revealed about Himself in His Word with childlike faith.

Second, we must seek to know the Lord through *humble repentance*. God is God. To know Him rightly is to fear Him (Prov. 2:5; 9:10). In the fear of God, we must hate sin, turn away from it (Job 28:28), and turn to Him in love (Deut. 10:12). Without knowing ourselves in our sinfulness and need, we cannot know God in His holiness and grace.

Third, we must seek to know the Lord through *Christ-centered faith*. Jesus declared Himself to be "the way, the *truth*, and the life." He Himself makes known the unseen God (John 1:18; 14:6–9). Faith is not simply the initial act of taking hold of Christ at the beginning of the Christian life. We must continue in Christ-centered faith throughout the Christian life (Col. 2:6; Gal. 2:20).

Fourth, we must seek to know God through *righteous action*. We are not saved by our works, but by grace alone.

However, this grace *works* to make us a new creation "in Christ Jesus unto good works, which God hath before ordained that we should walk in them" (Eph. 2:8–10). This means we must become hearers and doers of the Word (James 1:22–25). Personal knowledge of God deepens as we walk with Him in love and obedience.

Fifth, we must seek to know God through *holy desire*. We must treat the knowledge of God as much more than *useful*; we must regard Him as supremely *beautiful* and *desirable* (Ps. 27:4). Jonathon Edwards considers "a direct view of the glorious things of the gospel" to be of "the sweetest joys and delights I have experienced."[3] Let us pray with Moses, "Shew me thy glory" (Ex. 33:18).

REFLECTION QUESTIONS

1. Do you regard knowing God as your greatest privilege? Have you entered into a true covenantal relationship with God through the grace of knowing Him?

2. When do you find yourself striving after worldly "wisdom," "might," or "riches" in the place of knowing God (Jer. 9:23–24)? What is the effect of such a pursuit in your life?

---

3. Jonathan Edwards, *Personal Narrative*, in *The Works of Jonathan Edwards* (New Haven, Conn.: Yale University Press, 1957–2008), 16:800.

3. In John 17:3, Jesus equates eternal life with knowing God. If you could be in heaven where there is pleasure, friends, no sickness, and no death—but Christ were not there—would you be satisfied? How does being with and knowing Christ make heaven truly to be heaven?

4. David prayed, "One thing have I desired of the LORD, that will I seek after; that I may dwell in the house of the LORD all the days of my life, to behold the beauty of the LORD, and to enquire in his temple" (Ps. 27:4). What has been and is presently the "one thing" you desire?

5. According to 1 John 2:3, how can you know that you truly know God (cf. John 14:21)?

6. Take a few minutes to meditate on the gracious fact that God wills to be known and takes the initiative to reveal Himself to us in our fallen, sinful state.

DIGGING DEEPER

- Some other Scripture passages about knowing God include Psalms 9:10; 27:4; Isaiah 43:10; 45:22; Hosea 6:6; Romans 1:21–25; 2 Peter 1:3–4; and John 14:21.

- Skeptics and agnostics would say that if there is a God, then He is so far above us that we cannot *know* Him—or that perhaps we might know something about God, but we cannot know Him personally. These statements would be true if theology were merely *our* human quest to discover God. However, Christian theology arises from *God's* pursuit of *us*. This is grace: God wills to be known (Isa. 45:22). He creates us in His image with the potential to know Him truly. By the grace of Christ, He "renews" us "in knowledge after the image" of God (Col. 3:10). And He reveals Himself to us through His works of creation and providence, and supremely through His incarnate Word Jesus Christ revealed in His inscripturated Word as applied by the Holy Spirit (1 Cor. 2:9–16).

- In the Gospel of John, Christ's words imply that the knowledge of God illuminates the minds of men and guides their lives (John 1:4; 8:12), engages their faith in Christ (3:15–16; 6:47), delivers them from perdition (3:15–16; 10:28), releases them from condemnation (3:36; 5:24), satisfies their deepest desires (4:14; 6:35), brings them into communion with the living God (5:26), and guarantees their future resurrection to eternal life (6:40; 11:25). What a marvelous gift is the knowledge of God through Jesus Christ!

- See also John Frame, *The Doctrine of the Knowledge of God: A Theology of Lordship* (Phillipsburg, N.J.: P&R, 1987); Joel R. Beeke and Paul Smalley, *Reformed Systematic Theology, Volume 1: Revelation and God* (Wheaton, Ill.: Crossway, 2019).

GOD'S NATURE AND ATTRIBUTES

3

SCRIPTURE MEDITATION

I will speak of the glorious honour of thy majesty, and of thy wondrous works. And men shall speak of the might of thy terrible acts: and I will declare thy greatness. They shall abundantly utter the memory of thy great goodness, and shall sing of thy righteousness. The LORD is gracious, and full of compassion; slow to anger, and of great mercy. The LORD is good to all: and his tender mercies are over all his works.
—PSALM 145:5–9

PRAYER

Heavenly Father, all Thy perfections—Thy greatness, eternality, sovereignty, power, goodness, compassion, patience, and love—are displayed in Thy Son, the God-man Christ Jesus. He is the brightness of Thy glory and the express image of Thy person. As I turn to meditate upon Thy attributes, turn my mind from self and enlarge my heart's ability to understand, in a personal way, the glory of Thy perfections— that I may adore, imitate, revere, love, and obey Thee better. In Jesus's name. Amen.

BIBLICAL PERSPECTIVE

Scripture often invites us to praise God's name: "I will praise thy name for ever and ever" (v. 2). The "name" of the Lord refers to all of God's "names, titles, attributes, ordinances, word, and works…anything whereby God maketh himself known"[1]—including all His revealed glory and fame. Psalm 76:1 says, "In Judah is God known: his name is great in Israel." The name of the Lord is His glory (Ex. 33:18–19; Ps. 102:15) and the object of prayer and worship (Gen. 4:26; Ps. 7:17).

So, how do we praise and extol the "name" of God in a proper, reverential, and biblical way? It is through the *attributes* that God has revealed about Himself. We bless God's name according to His *attributes*. God's attributes are qualities that are closely and permanently associated with Him, and that we use to identify Him and to express "the glory due unto his name" (Ps. 29:2). God's attributes have been a focus of the worship and piety of God's people throughout the centuries—as demonstrated in scriptural summaries of God's attributes and echoed in the confessions of the Christian church.

One of the most significant biblical summaries of God's attributes is the divine self-revelation that took place at Mount Sinai. Moses had prayed, "Shew me thy glory." The Lord told Moses, "I will make all my goodness pass before thee," but warned, "thou canst not see my face: for there shall no man see me, and live" (Ex. 33:18–20). The next

---

1. Westminster Shorter Catechism, Q. 54–55, in *Reformed Confessions of the 16th and 17th Centuries in English Translation: 1523–1693*, comp. James T. Dennison Jr. (Grand Rapids: Reformation Heritage Books, 2008–2014), 4:360.

morning, Moses hid in a cleft of rock and God passed by, proclaiming His glorious name:

> And the LORD passed by before him, and proclaimed, The LORD, The LORD God, merciful and gracious, longsuffering, and abundant in goodness and truth, keeping mercy for thousands, forgiving iniquity and transgression and sin, and that will by no means clear the guilty; visiting the iniquity of the fathers upon the children, and upon the children's children, unto the third and to the fourth generation. (Ex. 34:6–7)

Calvin called these words from Exodus 34 "as clear and satisfactory a description of the nature of God…as can anywhere be found."[2]

These attributes were declared by God after the *exodus* (as Moses interceded for the covenant-breaking Israelites after the sin of the golden calf) and were echoed by the Israelites after their return from the *exile* (which was the punishment for covenant-breaking):

> Stand up and bless the LORD your God for ever and ever: and blessed be thy glorious name, which is exalted above all blessing and praise…. Thou art a God ready to pardon, gracious and merciful, slow to anger, and of great kindness…the great, the mighty, and the terrible God, who keepest covenant and mercy. (Neh. 9:5, 17, 32)

Our biblical faith is therefore grounded in the attributes of our covenant-keeping God. God's attributes sharply distinguish Him from His creatures, rule out idolatry, and

---

2. Calvin, *Commentaries*, vol. 6 (Grand Rapids: Baker, 2003), on Ps. 145:8.

condemn the false worship of this world. These attributes provide definitive content to the heart knowledge of God's covenant people, they give color and clarity to worship, and they sparkle brilliantly in God's saving work in Christ. The study of God's attributes is the joy of His people, for it leads to the greatest of gifts: the knowledge of the Lord.

One helpful way we can categorize God's attributes is by the two broad categories of God's *greatness* and God's *goodness*. For instance, the psalmist invites us to praise "the glorious honour of thy majesty, and of thy wondrous works" and "the might of thy terrible acts [or, *awesome deeds*]." He thus extols God's name according to His attribute of *greatness* (Ps. 145:3–6). The psalmist then directs us to "utter the memory of thy great goodness, and shall sing of thy righteousness" (vv. 7–9). He thus praises God's name according to His attribute of *goodness*. The rest of Psalm 145 continues, alternating between praising the attributes of God's greatness (vv. 11–13) and goodness (vv. 14–21)—His *majesty* and His *mercy*. These paired concepts of God's greatness and goodness, *lordship* and *love*, or *majesty* and *moral excellence* are found in many other scriptural summaries of God's attributes (Ex. 34:6–7; Jer. 9:24–10:12; 1 Tim. 1:12–17).

God's attribute of *holiness* may be considered the glory of all His attributes. He is "the Holy One"—and thus incomparable (Isa. 40:25), but He is also "the Holy One of Israel"—the faithful Lord of His covenant people (Isa. 1:2–4). Holiness thus summarizes both the *majesty* and *moral excellence*—the greatness and goodness—of the divine nature. It also sets the experiential tone of reverential fear by which we should approach all God's attributes and works, and yet with the hope of His holy nearness to the contrite in heart (Isa. 57:15).

Meditating upon God's attributes leads us to the knowledge of God, yet on a human level, for we cannot penetrate the infinite depths of His glory or fully trace out His ways (Rom. 11:33). However, the Bible's statements do reveal truly who God is: "God is a Spirit" (John 4:24); "God is light" (1 John 1:5); "God is love" (4:8), and so on. Since these are words from God, we must believe them to be meaningful and true. Herman Bavinck said, "As God reveals himself, so he is."[3]

It is impossible to overstate the importance of making God's attributes the focus of our attention, affection, and admiration. Charles Spurgeon said,

> The word, the character, and the actions of God should be evermore before our eyes; we should learn, consider, and reverence them. Men forget what they do not wish to remember, but the excellent attributes of the Most High are objects of the believer's affectionate and delighted admiration.... This inner love to the right must be the main spring of Christian integrity in our public walk.[4]

Praise God that in Christ Jesus all the attributes of God have taken human form and have been directed toward our redemption, our re-creation in God's image, and the consummation of His kingdom!

---

3. Herman Bavinck, *Reformed Dogmatics*, ed. John Bolt, trans. John Vriend (Grand Rapids: Baker Academic, 2003–2008), 2:111.

4. C. H. Spurgeon, *The Treasury of David* (New York: Funk & Wagnalls Company, 1882), 1:273.

REFLECTION QUESTIONS

1. The Belgic Confession (art. 1) speaks of God in terms of His attributes or perfections: "We all believe with the heart and confess with the mouth that there is one only simple and spiritual Being, which we call God; and that He is eternal, incomprehensible, invisible, immutable, infinite, almighty, perfectly wise, just, good, and the overflowing fountain of all good." Which of these attributes relate more to God's greatness, and which relate more to His goodness?

2. How is God's holiness the glory of all His attributes? How does it summarize both His majesty and His moral excellence?

3. Spurgeon said that we know the name of God when we have "an experimental acquaintance with the attributes of God."[5] Which of God's attributes do you have an experiential acquaintance with, and how?

4. How does the classification of God's attributes as *lordship* and *love* (or *majesty* and *moral excellence*) tend to promote balanced biblical piety? Which aspect do you emphasize? How can you be more balanced?

---

5. C. H. Spurgeon, *The Treasury of David*, 1:110.

5. Which of God's attributes has been especially challenging for you to understand or apply in your life, perhaps as it relates to an area of trial, temptation, or sin?

6. Spurgeon said that every one of God's attributes are "anchors to hold the soul from drifting in seasons of peril."[6] Which attribute of God is especially important for you to meditate upon in your present situation? How can you take hold of God in this attribute by faith, adoration, and imitation?

DIGGING DEEPER

- Some other Scripture passages about God's attributes include Numbers 14:18; 2 Chronicles 30:9; Psalms 86:15; 99:1–5; 103:8; 111:4; 113:5; 116:5; Jeremiah 9:24; 10:6, 10, 12; Joel 2:13; Jonah 4:2; Nahum 1:3; and 1 Timothy 1:12–17; 6:15–16.

- From the earliest days of the church, the saints have confessed their faith in God according to the attributes of His divine nature. Tertullian wrote of God's supreme greatness (*summum magnum*), eternity, power, and uniqueness.[7] Augustine confessed "that the Creator both lives in the highest sense, and perceives and understands

---

6. C. H. Spurgeon, *The Treasury of David*, 1:110.

7. Tertullian, *Against Marcion*, 1.3, in *The Ante-Nicene* Fathers, ed. Alexander Roberts and James Donaldson (New York: Charles Scribner's Sons, 1918), 3:273.

all things, and that He cannot die, or suffer decay, or be changed; and that He is not a body, but a spirit, of all the most powerful, most righteous, most beautiful, most good, most blessed."[8]

• The most common distinction among Reformed theologians is that between God's *communicable* (for example, love, wisdom) and *incommunicable* (for example, omnipresence, eternity) attributes. But even with the communicable attributes, which God is able to share, God displays them in a way that infinitely transcends man's display of them. Humans have "wisdom," but God's wisdom infinitely transcends man's wisdom, involving an infinite, eternal, divine mode of knowing to which man's mind can never attain (Ps. 139:6; Isa. 40:13–14, 28; 55:8–9). Bavinck said, "Everyone admits that the communicable attributes in an absolute sense—as they exist in God—are just as incommunicable as the others."[9]

• See also A. W. Pink, *The Attributes of God* (Grand Rapids: Baker, 1975); Stephen Charnock, *The Existence and Attributes of God* in *Works*, vols. 1–2 (Edinburgh: Banner of Truth, 2010); William Bates, *The Harmony of the Divine Attributes* (London: J. Darby, 1674; repr., Port St. Lucie, Fla.: Solid Ground Christian Books, 2010).

---

8. Augustine, *On the Trinity*, 15.4.6, in *A Select Library of Nicene and Post-Nicene Fathers of the Christian Church*, ed. Philip Schaff (New York: Christian Literature, 1888), 3:202.

9. Bavinck, *Reformed Dogmatics*, 2:132.

GOD IS GOD

4

SCRIPTURE MEDITATION

Be still, and know that I am God: I will be exalted among the heathen, I will be exalted in the earth.

—PSALM 46:10

PRAYER

Gracious Lord, Thou art God and I am not. Thou art infinite and I am finite. Thou art powerful and I am weak. As I meditate upon Thy character, apply the truths of Thy Word to my life by Thy Spirit. Bring to my mind areas in my life that need change, encouragement, and peace. I desire to exalt Thee now as I meditate on the truth that Thou art not just the God of the universe—eternal and sovereign—but *my* God. As Thy sheep, I come to Thee, my Shepherd, in search of green pastures and still waters; restore my soul. In Christ's name I pray. Amen.

BIBLICAL PERSPECTIVE

"In God we Trust" is printed on the back of every U.S. dollar bill (at least for now). But *who* is the God we "trust"? And who are the "we" who trust that God? Many people believe that the God of the Christian faith is the same God as the god of the Islamic faith or the Hindu faith or any number of other religions. But the God of Scripture—the true and living God—is altogether different.

One of the fundamental differences is that we believe in the God who eternally exists as three persons, as God the *Trinity*: God the Father, God the Son, and God the Holy Spirit. These three persons share the same essence and enjoy perfect unity forever (Heb. 1:3). None is greater than the other and none is inferior, and they are not three gods. He is one God (Deut. 6:4), who exists in three persons forever (Matt. 28:19; 2 Cor. 13:14).

In Psalm 46:10, God exhorts His people: "Be still, and know that I am God." The context is one of God bringing battle and war to an end. He then turns from the indicative—what He's done—to the imperative—what He requires of His people. "Be still," then can be viewed as a ceasing from battle. As you meditate on this verse, there are a few things to keep in mind.

First, this isn't simply a good suggestion; it's a *command*! In other words, this is a matter of obedience to God. But as much as it brings God glory, we partake of Him in this delightful duty.

Second, God tells us to "be still." As mentioned, the context is one of battle. But how may this apply to you? Is there a sense in which you are "fighting" for reputation, significance, or any number of selfish endeavors? Indeed, stillness is a resting from sin and a resting in God in the midst of busy schedules. Between family, school, jobs, sports, hobbies, and friends, being still seems very unfamiliar to many of us. The world is continually enticing us to fill our schedules and calendars with more and more. In addition, the idea of a Sabbath rest on the Lord's Day (Sunday) has virtually been lost in the dust of cleaning the house, homework, or football. We need to hear this message of stillness before a holy and gracious God.

Third, we are commanded to "know" something about God. The kind of knowing here isn't an empty knowledge, but a faith-filled, loving knowledge. In the New Testament, Paul prays for the Philippian church by saying, "And this I pray, that your love may abound yet more and more in knowledge and in all judgment" (Phil. 1:9). Even the demons believe and know that God is God (James 2:19), but God calls us to a knowledge of Him that draws our affections and faith together into a life that glorifies and exalts Him.

Fourth, God tells us to know that He is *God*. According to the Bible, this means that He is perfectly and completely sovereign, holy, wise, just, good, gracious, loving, and faithful (among many other characteristics). And He commands us to *know* Him. Jesus echoed this when He prayed, "And this is life eternal, that they might know thee the only true God, and Jesus Christ, whom thou hast sent" (John 17:3).

Finally, Psalm 46:10 tells us that God will be exalted among the nations and in the earth. This not only happened in its immediate Jewish context, but has continued to happen down through the ages and will find its final expression when we gather around the heavenly throne as people "of all nations, and kindreds, and people, and tongues" (Rev. 7:9).

God the Father planned our redemption. God the Son accomplished our redemption. God the Holy Spirit applies our redemption. Though we deserve death as the payment of our sin (Rom. 6:23), God is gracious and has sent His only Son to be our substitute on the cross. Though we have been spared eternal separation from God, He did not spare His own Son, but gave Him up for us all (Rom. 8:32).

REFLECTION QUESTIONS

1. What are some initial thoughts that come to your mind when you think of the phrase, "God is God"?

2. What do you think Luther meant when he said, "Letting God be God is more than half of all true religion"?

3. This passage tells us to "be still." Do you find that your life is too busy? Do you find it difficult to spend time with God, to read His Word, or to pray? Are there activities that you could cut out for a season?

4. What are some things that you could do to increase your knowledge of and love for God? Are you willing to make these things a priority in your daily life? How?

5. How might the sin of pride hinder your recognition that God is God?

6. What do you think it means to "exalt" God at school, at work, or in your home?

7. How is it that God can say with full confidence, "I *will* be exalted"? What is at least one thing this says about His character?

DIGGING DEEPER

- Some other Scripture passages on the Godhood of God include Deuteronomy 4:35; 32:39; Psalms 18:31; 100:3; Isaiah 44:6; 45:5; Joel 2:27.

- That God exists as three persons in one Godhead rightly points to the truth that He is *relational*. Genesis 1:27 says that we are created "in his image," which means (in part) that we are created for relationship—with God and with others. The unity of the community that we share with one another as the church should reflect the unity of the community of the Trinity.

- The development of Trinitarian theology took center stage over the first five centuries of the Christian church. The result of these labors can be found in confessions like the Nicene Creed (325/381 AD) or the Chalcedonian Creed (451 AD).

- Many people today want to say that God is *only* loving or *only* gracious. But God is *perfectly* loving and *perfectly* gracious. He is also *perfectly* just and *perfectly* holy. We cannot limit God's attributes to a few things we think are nice. Rather, we must adjust our thinking and pattern our minds after God's Word.

- See also Gerald Bray, *The Doctrine of God* (Downers Grove, Ill.: InterVarsity Press, 1993); R. C. Sproul, *The Character of God: Discovering the God Who Is* (Ventura, Calif.: Regal, 1995).

GOD'S NAME IS "THE LORD" (YHWH)

5

SCRIPTURE MEDITATION

And God said unto Moses, I AM THAT I AM: and he said, Thus shalt thou say unto the children of Israel, I AM hath sent me unto you. And God said moreover unto Moses, Thus shalt thou say unto the children of Israel, the LORD God of your fathers, the God of Abraham, the God of Isaac, and the God of Jacob, hath sent me unto you: this is my name for ever, and this is my memorial unto all generations.
—EXODUS 3:14–15

PRAYER

Ever-faithful, covenant-keeping Lord in heaven, hallowed be Thy name. Thy name declares Thy majesty and Thy mercy. Thou art high and lifted up, yet Thou dwellest with the humble and contrite in heart. As I turn to meditate upon Thy great name "The LORD," expose any tendency in me that does not rest in Thy covenant promises, that asserts itself against Thy will, and that stifles a clear apprehension of Thy truth. May Thy name instill in me a fear and love of Thee that bears fruit unto Thy glory. I pray this in the strong name of the Savior. Amen.

BIBLICAL PERSPECTIVE

Decades after Moses had fled as a fugitive from Pharaoh, he led his father-in-law's flock through the rocky desert of Sinai. At Mount Horeb, Moses saw a bush that burned with fire but was not consumed by it. Drawn to it by curiosity, he was shocked to hear the voice of God speaking from the midst of the flames. God spoke to Moses about His compassion for the children of Israel and His intent to rescue them from slavery. God commissioned him to go to Pharaoh and lead Israel out of Egypt. Moses asked for the name of the One who sent him. God replied, "I AM THAT I AM: and he said, Thus shalt thou say unto the children of Israel, I AM hath sent me unto you" (Ex. 3:14). Thus God revealed His name "I AM," translated "the LORD," to Moses.

When does God reveal His name "I AM" in the Bible? He reveals it especially when He is about to redeem His people. Therefore, God's name "I AM" should forever remind us of God's gracious initiative to save His people—from the time of Israel's first Passover, to its fulfillment in Christ's work of eternal salvation as our true Passover lamb (1 Cor. 5:7), who redeemed people out of every nation (Rev. 5:6, 9).

The divine name that God revealed to Moses is expanded in two ways: "I AM THAT I AM," revealing God's sovereign lordship (Ex. 3:14)—and "I AM with you" (v. 12), revealing His covenantal faithfulness.

First, God's name "the LORD"—expanded to "I AM THAT I AM" or "I will be"—reveals His sovereign Lordship. "I AM" speaks of God's absolute being and implies God's self-existence and independence as the only God. "I will be" suggests that God's dealings with Moses and Israel are not subject to time, but He is free to exercise His sovereign lordship over time. He has always been and will always be Lord. So when we come to God for grace, we can rest confidently in His sovereign freedom to bestow grace upon us (Ex. 33:19; Rom. 9:15–18).

Second, God's name "the LORD"—expanded to "I will be with you"—reveals His covenant faithfulness (3:12; 4:12, 15). God repeatedly affirms His compassion for His suffering people and His intention to save them (Ex. 2:24–25; 3:7–10, 16–17). God then connects His name "I AM" with "the LORD God of your fathers, the God of Abraham, the God of Isaac, and the God of Jacob" (3:14–15). God is giving Abraham's offspring salvation and inheritance because He keeps His covenant promises. When you trust God as your *covenant* Lord, you also glorify Him as your *sovereign* Lord.

The twofold significance of God's name means that God's sovereignty does not hold Him back from a personal relationship with you. You should never think that God's transcendent glory as the LORD inhibits His compassionate faithfulness to His people. God's lordship over the world means that He controls all things, whether pharaohs or frogs, to fulfill the words of His covenant. On the other hand, God's covenantal faithfulness teaches us to view Him not as a frighteningly arbitrary and chaotic power, but as a personal, righteous God worthy of our absolute trust and fervent hope. Let us rely on God's covenant *precisely because* He is sovereign.

Let us also consider that God's name "the LORD" points us to His Trinitarian nature. The Trinity—the Father, the Son, and the Holy Spirit—is the sovereign, eternal "I AM." God the Son and God the Spirit share in the one

divine "name" of the Father (Matt. 28:19). Christ identified Himself as the Lord who appeared to Moses, for He
said, "Before Abraham was, I am" (John 8:56, 58). The most
basic confession of the Christian faith is that "Jesus Christ
is Lord" (Phil. 2:10–11; cf. Isa. 45:21–23). Likewise, the Holy
Spirit is also "the LORD" (Isa. 63:11–14; Jer. 31:33–34; Heb.
10:15–17). In all three divine persons, the Father, the Son
sent by the Father, and the Spirit of the Son sent by the
Father, we encounter the one covenant Lord who draws us
into reverent and loving relationship with Himself (Gal.
4:4–6; Eph. 3:14–21).

The name of the Lord thus stands at the heart of the
gospel, for we must know and call upon His name to be
saved (Acts 2:21; Rom. 10:13). Let us, therefore, humble
ourselves with holy awe in the presence of the great "I
AM." Let us consider His absolute independence from all
limitations and His constant faithfulness to His covenant.
Let us worship Him with joy and trembling. Let us trust
Him wholeheartedly as our only Redeemer. In the divine
name, "the LORD," we find the root from which grow all
the sweet fruits that nourish the believer's soul in every trial
and temptation.

REFLECTION QUESTIONS

1. With what two phrases in Exodus 3 did God explain the meaning of "I AM"?

2. How does God's name reveal His independent, eternal being? How does it reveal His faithful presence with His people?

3. Why is the redemptive context of the revelation of God's name in Exodus 3 important for you today?

4. Proverbs 18:10 says, "The name of the LORD is a strong tower: the righteous runneth into it, and is safe." What have you learned about God's name from reading this chapter that reminds you that you can safely hide yourself in Him?

5. Why is it important to embrace both the sovereign independence and the faithful presence of the Lord in order to maintain a balanced, biblical piety?

DIGGING DEEPER

- Some other Scripture passages on God's name "the LORD" include Exodus 7:5; Psalm 135:1, 3, 13; Isaiah 41:4; Romans 10:9, 13; 1 Corinthians 12:3; and Revelation 1:8.

- Just as the Lord expounded the covenantal aspect of His name "I AM" by saying, "I am with you," so Christ expounded the grace of His name by His many "I am" (*ego eimi*) sayings recorded in the Gospel of John. The Lord Jesus declared, "I am the bread of life" (John 6:35), "I am the light of the world" (8:12), "I am the door" (10:7, 9), "I am the good shepherd" (10:11, 14), "I am the resurrection, and the life" (11:25), "I am the way, the truth, and the life: no man cometh unto the Father, but by me" (14:6), and, "I am the vine, ye are the branches… without me ye can do nothing" (15:5).

- The pronunciation of the name *YHWH*, called the *Tetragrammaton* for its four Hebrew letters, is uncertain. For hundreds of years, it has been rendered by Christian scholars as "Jehovah." Many modern scholars regard Jehovah as the result of the addition of the vowels from "Lord" (*'Adonai*) or the Aramaic word for "name" (*shem'a*) to the consonants of YHWH. They argue, however, for the pronunciation "Yahweh." This pronunciation is supported by Patristic testimony and a Greek translation of Samaritan writings.

- See also Terry L. Johnson, *The Identity and Attributes of God* (Edinburgh: Banner of Truth, 2019).

GOD IS HOLY

6

SCRIPTURE MEDITATION

And they sing the song of Moses the servant of God, and the song of the Lamb, saying, Great and marvellous are thy works, Lord God Almighty; just and true are thy ways, thou King of saints. Who shall not fear thee, O Lord, and glorify thy name? for thou only art holy: for all nations shall come and worship before thee; for thy judgments are made manifest.

—REVELATION 15:3–4

PRAYER

Gracious Triune God, there is none like Thee. Thou alone art high and lifted up and worthy of my worship. Indeed, Thou art holy, holy, holy. As Thy child, please tune my heart toward Thine, and shape my mind by the power of Thy Word. Be pleased with the meditation of my soul, for Christ's sake. Amen.

BIBLICAL PERSPECTIVE

Can you think of a time when you have been the stranger? Or maybe you might be able to think of a time when you have felt completely different from other people? Similarly, God is altogether different from us. He is in complete control; we are not. He is perfect and righteous; we are not. He is God; we are not.

The holiness of God points to two specific elements of God's character. First, it points to the fact that God is fully set apart and different from anything and anyone else. Second, it points to the fact that He is morally righteous in His manifold perfections. In Genesis 2:3, God set apart the seventh day as "holy," which means it was to be *different* from all the other days. In Exodus 3:5, God tells Moses that the ground on which he stood was "holy" ground, which means that it was set apart and *different*. Paul tells Timothy that whoever is cleansed from sin is "sanctified" (2 Tim. 2:21). Being holy, in the first place, then, means that God is altogether different and set apart in glory, power, wisdom, righteousness, authority, goodness, love, truth, grace, and knowledge.

But holiness also refers to God's perfect, righteous character. A. W. Pink explains, "The sum of all moral excellency is found in him."[1] No other purity comes close to the purity of God. He holds the full measure of all that is good and right. Every act, thought, and intent of God is completely righteous and perfect. He does not err or fail, nor does He act unjustly toward His creation. God's commandments, too, are holy. They are perfect, right, and true. They are different from the law of man, for they are derived from a holy and righteous God.

In Isaiah 6, the prophet records the seraphim calling out, "Holy, holy, holy, is the LORD of hosts: the whole earth is full of his glory" (Isa. 6:3). Likewise, the apostle John writes

---

1. A. W. Pink, *The Attributes of God* (Grand Rapids: Baker, 1975), 41.

of the heavenly courts of praise: "Holy, holy, holy, LORD God Almighty, which was, and is, and is to come" (Rev. 4:8). The repetition expresses the superlative—as in high, higher, highest. That the biblical writers attest to the thrice-holy God is an explicit reference that there exists no one like God. He is altogether different and set apart, while manifesting the full sum of moral perfection.

Not only is God holy, but He calls us to holiness—perfect moral obedience (Lev. 11:44; 1 Peter 1:15). Many people today think that God simply wants us to try our hardest. But that is not a biblical concept of the Christian life. God's standard for us is absolute perfection. Jesus explained, "Be ye therefore perfect, even as your Father which is in heaven is perfect" (Matt. 5:48). God doesn't grade on a curve; He calls us to His standard of perfection and holiness. "But there's no way anyone can be saved!" you might be thinking. Ah, but there is a way—*the* Way, the Truth, and the Life (John 14:6). What's impossible for man is possible with God.

While we are called to perfect holiness, we have fallen short of this glory of God (Rom. 3:23), and the wages of our sin is death (Rom. 6:23). Because God is holy, He must punish sin. Sin cannot stand for one second before a holy and righteous God. In fact, one of the most fundamental questions of life is: "How can an unholy sinner stand in the presence of a holy God?"

But God, who is rich in mercy, sent His only Son into this world to become our substitute (Eph. 2:4). All of our filthiness, sin, blemishes, and unholiness was placed on Christ and He nailed it to the cross, thereby canceling the record of debt that stood against us (Col. 2:14). In return, the perfect record of Jesus's double obedience—His passive obedience to pay for our sin completely and His active obedience to obey the law perfectly on our behalf—was credited to our account. By faith, we are so unified with Him that when God looks upon us, He sees the righteousness and the holy record of His own Son, Jesus Christ.

REFLECTION QUESTIONS

1. In Revelation 15, the apostle John imparts a vision of heavenly worship around the throne. The heartbeat of this worship is the "song of the Lamb." Why do you think the sacrificial lambs in the Old Testament (cf. Lev. 1:3) had to be "without blemish" to atone (temporarily) for the sins of God's people?

2. How do those Old Testament "unblemished lambs" point to *the* Lamb of God, Jesus Christ?

3. How does God being "just and true" (v. 3) relate to God being holy?

4. How do God's "judgments" (v. 4) relate to God being holy?

5. When you think of God being holy, what comes to mind about yourself? Does the thought of God's holiness evoke any immediate response in your heart?

6. Throughout Paul's epistles, he calls various Christians "saints," which in the Greek literally means *holy ones*. If we are not—in and of ourselves—holy, then how can Paul call imperfect, unholy believers "holy"?

DIGGING DEEPER

- Other Scripture passages on the holiness of God include Exodus 15:11; Leviticus 11:44; 2 Chronicles 20:21; Psalms 30:4; 89:35; 110:3; 145:17; Isaiah 6:3; Mark 1:24; 1 Peter 1:15; and Revelation 4:8.

- The sacraments (baptism and the Lord's Supper) are examples of something that is holy that we partake of in the Christian life. In fact, part of the word "sacred" is derived from an understanding of holiness.

- Another clear example of something set apart is the Bible, God's *holy* Word. God's Word is unlike any other book. It is fully inspired by the Holy Spirit and, therefore, comes ultimately from a divine author (2 Tim. 3:16; 2 Peter 1:21). Being "holy" would appropriately refer to it being wholly different, set apart, true, and right.

- See also R. C. Sproul, *The Holiness of God* (Carol Stream, Ill.: Tyndale House Publishers, 2000).

GOD IS SPIRIT

7

SCRIPTURE MEDITATION

But the hour cometh, and now is, when the true worshippers shall worship the Father in spirit and in truth: for the Father seeketh such to worship him. God is a Spirit: and they that worship him must worship him in spirit and in truth.

—JOHN 4:23–24

PRAYER

Heavenly Father, I thank Thee that Thou hast revealed Thyself as Spirit that we may know Thy power, vitality, and personality. Forgive and cleanse me from my sins that contradict Thy spirituality— my pride, self-righteousness, envy, and greed. Teach me to worship Thee in accord with Thy spirituality— in spirit and in truth—sincerely, reverently, and from my full being. And let the truth that Thou art Spirit yield spiritual fruit in my life. I pray this in Jesus's name. Amen.

BIBLICAL PERSPECTIVE

In Jesus's conversation with the Samaritan woman, He offered her what she desperately needed—the "living water" of life in Him (John 4:10). She also needed to repent of her sin, Jesus said. Uncomfortable with facing her inner need, the woman evaded the issue of her sin and brought up a politically charged question of where the Samaritans ought to worship. But Jesus steered the conversation back to the main issue of God's will for her: "the hour cometh, when ye shall neither in this mountain, nor yet at Jerusalem, worship the Father.... God is a Spirit: and they that worship him must worship him in spirit and in truth" (vv. 21, 24). The main issue at hand—for the Samaritan woman and for us—is the spirituality of God and its practical implication for us to worship God properly: in spirit and in truth.

What did Christ mean by saying "God is Spirit" (NKJV)? Christ was teaching us that God is "immortal, wise and understanding, simple, invisible, and incorporeal."[1] God is, in the words of the Westminster Confession (2.1), "a most pure spirit," or a supremely spiritual Spirit.[2] As such, He is a Spirit like no other.

In the biblical story, God reveals that His nature is "spirit." God forbade the Israelites from representing His presence with an image or a bodily shape (Ex. 20:4). The Lord manifested His presence in the tabernacle, and later in the temple, by a fiery, glorious cloud (Ex. 40:34–38; 1 Kings 8:10–11); and yet, God was not bound to the temple: "behold, the heaven and heaven of heavens cannot contain thee" (1 Kings 8:27). The saints of the Old Testament

---

1. Arthur Hildersham, *Lectures upon the Fourth of John* (London: by G. M. for Edward Brewster, 1629), 189.

2. *Reformed Confessions*, 4:236. See the *London Baptist Confession* (2.1), in *Reformed Confessions*, 4:535.

understood that God is not an embodied or localized being, but an infinite and glorious Spirit.

When Jesus Christ came and abolished the earthly temple so that His people would be the living temple of the Father, Son, and Spirit, this was the supreme revelation that God is Spirit (1 Cor. 3:16; 1 Peter 2:5). God's presence is not visible to the eye, but His presence exercises powerful, invigorating effects upon the personality, character, and relationships of His people.

Let us consider several dimensions of God's spirituality. First, that "God is Spirit" teaches us about God's *incorporeality*: He has no physical body. Isaiah 31:3 expresses this contrast: "Now the Egyptians are men, and not God; and their horses flesh, and not spirit." People may imagine God to be an old man in the sky, but this is idolatrous: "His spiritual nature forbids our imagining anything earthly or carnal [fleshly] of him."[3] Our worship, too, must not be focused on locations or elaborate rituals, but we must approach God with repentance, spiritual obedience, and justice (Ps. 51:17; Isa. 1:11–20; Hos. 6:6). Our spiritual focus in worship should be on the Lamb of God who came to earth to atone for our sin and to be the new meeting place between God and man (John 1:29; 2:19–21).

Second, the fact that "God is Spirit" implies that human eyes cannot see God. When God reveals Himself to us, He does so through created means, not by a direct appearance of His being. Consequently, we depend on the voluntary self-disclosures of the *invisible* God. We perceive God "by

---

3. Calvin, *Institutes of the Christian Religion,* ed. John T. McNeill, trans. Ford Lewis Battles (Philadelphia: Westminster, 1960), 1.13.1.

faith...seeing him who is invisible" (Heb. 11:27). You can take hold of God by the "evidence" of faith as He reveals Himself in His *inscripturated* Word (Heb. 11:1) and in His *incarnate* Word, Jesus Christ (John 1:14; 14:9). God's invisibility is itself a revelation of His glory and spirituality, for it distinguishes Him from us and our world.

Third, Christ's words "God is Spirit" convey God's *intelligent personality*. God is not an impersonal force, but a personal, conscious being with knowledge, will, and affection. The Father "seeketh" true worshipers—implying God's *purpose* and *desire* which must be met with our personal faith response: "in spirit and in truth" (John 4:23–24). Since God is a personal, intelligent, and affectionate Spirit, we worship Him rightly only when, enabled by Christ, we do so in a personal, intelligent, and affectionate manner (Luke 1:46–47).

Fourth, the fact that "God is Spirit" communicates His *powerful vitality*. The word translated as "spirit" (*pneuma*) communicates energy and motion, indicating life (John 3:8; 6:63). God is constantly active; He is *pure actuality*. The water Jesus offers the Samaritan woman is *living*, so that it becomes in a person "a well of water springing up into everlasting life" (John 4:10, 14). Jesus means that God has life in Himself, gives life to all living things, and is the only one who can satisfy our spirits.

God's spirituality is therefore immensely practical. First, it exposes the lie of idol worship and exhorts us to turn "from idols to serve the living and true God" (1 Thess. 1:9). Second, God's spirituality demands simplicity in the worship of God in spirit and truth—we read the Word, pray the Word, sing the Word, preach the Word, and see the Word made visible in baptism and the Lord's Supper. Third, God's spirituality calls for worship marked by sincerity and understanding. We must watch and pray over our hearts, engage our minds, and consciously and reverently set ourselves in the presence of the awesome God. We must rid our worship of whatever does not honor God as personal and spiritual: empty traditionalism, superficial emotionalism, and desperate innovation and sensationalism. Finally, we must bear spiritual fruit as true worshipers. To know the living God is to have an inward fountain of eternal life springing up in one's soul (John 4:14; 7:37; 17:3) and to guard our hearts from sins of the soul such as pride, envy, malice, greed, wicked desires, self-righteousness, and covetousness. May the truth of God's spirituality cultivate true spirituality in your life.

REFLECTION QUESTIONS

1. How should God's spirituality and invisibility make Christ's incarnation exceedingly precious to us? Why should they cause us to treasure and study the Holy Scriptures?

2. How should God's spirituality cause us to reverence Him as transcendent, powerful, and distinct from us?

3. How should God's spirituality cause us to rejoice in His nearness and covenantal presence?

4. What are some ways in which we sin against God's spirituality in our worship? During worship, what changes in your heart or in your church can be made to better honor God as personal and spiritual?

5. When you think of God's spirituality, what particular "sins of the soul" in your life does this attribute of God challenge?

DIGGING DEEPER

- Some other Scripture passages on the spirituality of God include Genesis 1:1; Exodus 20:4–6; 40:34–38; Deuteronomy 4:11–19; 2 Chronicles 32:8; Job 9:11; Psalm 139:7; Jeremiah 10:14; 17:5; 23:23–24; Habakkuk 2:18; Acts 17:29; Romans 1:20; 1 Corinthians 3:16; Colossians 1:15; 1 Timothy 1:17; 6:16; and 1 Peter 2:5.

- Anthropomorphism[4] for God appears when the Bible describes Him as if He had a human constitution of body and spirit. God's "hand" and "arm" serve as metaphors for His power as Creator and Savior (Ps. 139:10; Isa. 52:10). God's "finger" can represent the work of His

---

4. Anthropomorphism: human characteristics attributed to God.

Spirit (Matt. 12:28; Luke 11:20). God's "eyes" function
as a figure of speech for His knowledge and providence
(2 Chron. 16:9); they cannot be physical eyes because
they are in every place (Prov. 15:3). God's "heart" and
"soul" represent His thoughts and affections (1 Kings
9:3; Ps. 11:5). Anthropomorphic language communicates
important truth about God, but we must not dishonor
God with creaturely limitations. Rather, we must
interpret anthropomorphisms in light of the revealed
attributes of God. Charnock said that just as the sun's
radiation could destroy us, but when filtered through our
atmosphere, it illuminates and warms us, so God con-
descends to reveal Himself in human terms so that His
glory will not harm us, but rather heal and help us.[5]

• See also Henry Scougal, *The Life of God in the Soul of Man:
Real Religion* (Fearn, Rosshire: Christian Focus, 2012);
Spirit & Truth: A Film about Worship, directed by Les
Lanphere (Port Saint Lucie, Fla.: Broken Stone Studio,
2019), DVD.

---

5. Stephen Charnock, *The Existence and Attributes of God* (1853; repr.,
Grand Rapids: Baker, 1996), 1:199.

8

GOD IS SIMPLE

SCRIPTURE MEDITATION

Hear, O Israel: The LORD our God is one LORD: and thou shalt love the LORD thy God with all thine heart, and with all thy soul, and with all thy might.

—DEUTERONOMY 6:4–5

PRAYER

Ever blessed Lord of lords, I praise Thee that Thou art not divided, but that all Thy attributes are fully present in Thy being at every moment, and that Thou *art* Thy attributes. As I turn to meditate upon the doctrine of Thy divine simplicity, impress upon my mind and heart the truth that the cross of Christ— the climax of Thy redemptive work—is where Thy simplicity shines forth the brightest, where all Thy attributes are on display, and where Thy Son magnifies the unity of all Thou art. I pray this in Jesus Christ's glorious name. Amen.

BIBLICAL PERSPECTIVE

Many Christians today may deny God's simplicity because of the negative connotation that the word "simple" has in everyday language.[1] However, divine simplicity means that God is perfect unity, without composition or division.[2] God is not composed of parts, for "a part is anything in a subject that is less than the whole and without which the subject would be really different than it is."[3] Therefore, God's simplicity means that His attributes and essence are all one in Him.[4]

We may start our thinking about God's simplicity with Christ's statement, "God is a Spirit" (John 4:24). Christ did not say that God *has* a spirit, but "God *is* a Spirit." Similarly, God does not *have* light or *love*, but "God *is* light" and "God *is* love" (1 John 1:5; 4:8, 16). These expressions do not declare parts of Him, but the whole of Him. God's essential act of love is Himself, for to love is to will good for someone, and "the good that He wills for Himself, is no other than Himself," as Thomas Aquinas put it.[5]

God's attributes *are* God. God's faithfulness is God. God's kindness is God. God's justice is God. Furthermore, the Scriptures do not say that God is partly spirit, partly light, and partly love, but God is spirit, God is light, and

---

1. Mark Jones, *God Is: A Devotional Guide to the Attributes of God* (Wheaton, Ill.: Crossway, 2017), 31.

2. William Perkins, *An Exposition of the Symbol*, in *The Works of William Perkins* (Grand Rapids: Reformation Heritage Books, 2017), 5:19.

3. James E. Dolezal, *All That Is in God: Evangelical Theology and the Challenge of Classical Christian Theism* (Grand Rapids: Reformation Heritage Books, 2017), 40.

4. A. A. Hodge, *Outlines of Theology* (1879; repr., Grand Rapids: Zondervan, 1972), 136.

5. Thomas Aquinas, *Summa Theologica*, trans. Fathers of the English Dominican Province (London: R & T Washbourne, 1914), *Pt. 1*, Q. 20, Art. 1, Reply Obj. 3.

God is love—implying that each of these words summarizes the whole of God's being. God's attributes, then, unite in His being. Each of His attributes qualifies the others, so that His power is "eternal power" (Rom. 1:20), and in His love He "loveth righteousness" (Ps. 33:5).[6]

Here are three ways that God's simplicity is richly practical. First, divine simplicity gives us assurance that wherever God is present, He is fully present with all His attributes.[7] God's perfections are not diffused or diluted throughout space or separable from one another. Therefore, we must fear Him, for *all of God* is always with us. We constantly dwell in the presence of the infinite, eternal, and unchangeable God of wisdom, power, justice, and love. This also engenders hope. We may call upon Him through Christ with complete confidence that *all of God is with His children* for their good.

Second, divine simplicity promotes sincere evangelical holiness and love. When the Lord revealed His simplicity in statements such as "God is light" and "God is love," He did not place them in theoretical discourses, but in admonitions to practical Christian living. Consider these statements in their contexts: "God is light, and in him is no darkness at all. If we say that we have fellowship with him, and walk in darkness, we lie, and do not the truth" (1 John 1:5–6); "Beloved, let us love one another: for love is of God; and

---

6. John Owen, *Vindiciae Evangelicae: Or, The Mystery of the Gospel Vindicated and Socinianism Examined*, in *The Works of John Owen,* ed. William H. Goold, 16 vols. (1850–1853; repr., Edinburgh: Banner of Truth, 1965–1968), 12:72.

7. Thomas C. Oden, *Systematic Theology: Volume 1, The Living God* (San Francisco: Harper and Row, 1987), 1:57.

every one that loveth is born of God, and knoweth God. He that loveth not knoweth not God; for God is love" (1 John 4:7–8). John is not encouraging "speculations about God's hidden essence," but he is helping us "to distinguish those who truly know God from those who falsely claim to know him."[8] The knowledge of God's simplicity, then, stimulates Christian sincerity. God is so completely identified with His light and love that it is impossible to know Him without walking in light and love. Let us demonstrate that we know God by walking with Him and becoming like Him.

A life characterized by "simplicity and godly sincerity" lays a foundation for a good conscience before God (2 Cor. 1:12). God's simplicity forms the point of integration for all Christian virtue. Let us pursue wholehearted trust in God and sincerity in godliness in our dealings with men as opposed to double-mindedness.[9]

Third, divine simplicity means that no fruit of the Spirit can be separated from any other in the image of God. There is profound unity in holiness, for it faintly reflects the simplicity of God. Love is patient and kind; love is humble; love is joyful, righteous, and true; love is strong to endure through all things (1 Cor. 13:4–7). Self-control and slowness to anger are real power, greater than the power of a conquering warrior (Prov. 16:32; 25:28). We cannot pursue love while neglecting patience and self-control (Gal.

---

8. Greg Nichols, *Lectures in Systematic Theology, Volume 1, Doctrine of God*, ed. Rob Ventura (Seattle: CreateSpace Independent Publishing Platform, 2017), 1:170.

9. Petrus van Mastricht, *Theoretical-Practical Theology, Volume 2: Faith in the Triune God* (Grand Rapids: Reformation Heritage Books, 2019), 147–53.

5:22–23). We cannot abound in love without also growing in knowledge and discernment (Phil. 1:9). Let us, therefore, pursue holistic godliness, for that is Godlikeness.

REFLECTION QUESTIONS

1. How would you explain God's attribute of divine simplicity to someone who asks what it means?

2. Do you believe that the Bible's statements that God is spirit, light, and love teach divine simplicity? Why or why not?

3. Meditate on the fact that you stand in the presence of *all* of God's attributes, not part of His attributes at any given moment but all of Him. How does this reality affect you?

4. Which of the applications in this chapter is most relevant to you in this season of your life? How can you make use of God's simplicity for your comfort and holiness?

5. Meditate on the application that you cannot pursue love while neglecting patience or self-control (Gal. 5:22–23), and neither can you abound in love without growing in knowledge and discernment (Phil. 1:9). How does this apply in your life right now?

DIGGING DEEPER

- Some other Scripture passages about God's simplicity include Deuteronomy 6:4; Jeremiah 23:6; Zechariah 14:9; Romans 8:10; 1 Corinthians 8:4; 1 Timothy 2:5; and James 1:17.

- The doctrine of divine simplicity is part of the theological legacy of the ancient church. Irenaeus said, "He is a simple, uncompounded Being, without diverse members, and altogether like, and equal to Himself, since He is wholly understanding, and wholly spirit, and wholly thought, and wholly intelligence, and wholly reason, and wholly hearing, and wholly seeing, and wholly light, and the whole source of all that is good."[10] Augustine said that "the nature of the Trinity is called simple, because it has not anything which it can lose, and because it is not one thing and its contents another, as a cup and the liquor, or a body and its color, or the air and the light or heat of it, or a mind and its wisdom."[11] See also the Belgic Confession (art. 1).

---

10. Irenaeus, *Against Heresies*, 2.13.3, in *ANF*, 1:374.
11. Augustine, *The City of God*, 11.10, in *NPNF*[1], 2:211.

- This simple God reveals Himself in the gospel as the triune God. God the Father is pure light without change or shadow (James 1:17). God the Son, incarnate in Jesus Christ, not only brings the light, He is the light (John 8:12). For those united to Him by a Spirit-worked faith, Christ is the way, the truth, and the life (14:6). He is our wisdom, righteousness, sanctification, and redemption (1 Cor. 1:30).

- See also Steven J. Duby, *Divine Simplicity: A Dogmatic Account* (New York: Bloomsbury T&T Clark, 2016); Petrus van Mastricht, *Theoretical-Practical Theology, Volume 2: Faith in the Triune God* (Grand Rapids: Reformation Heritage Books, 2019), 143–53; Mark Jones, *God Is* (Wheaton, Ill.: Crossway, 2019).

GOD IS TRIUNE

9

> *Peter, an apostle of Jesus Christ, to the strangers scat-*
> *tered throughout Pontus, Galatia, Cappadocia, Asia, and*
> *Bithynia, elect according to the foreknowledge of God the*
> *Father, through sanctification of the Spirit, unto obedience*
> *and sprinkling of the blood of Jesus Christ: grace unto you,*
> *and peace, be multiplied.*
>
> —1 PETER 1:1–2

PRAYER

Our God Most High, I praise Thee in Thy triune glory—Father, Son, and Holy Spirit. I thank Thee that all divine persons work for our salvation—the Father to send the Son and elect His people, the Son to accomplish redemption, and the Spirit to apply it. I need and love—and long to know better and love more—each of Thy divine persons. Let my heart glory in what Scripture has revealed about Thy triune nature; and about the things on which Scripture is silent, let my heart be silent in humble dependence upon Thee. May my meditation on Thy triune glory sanctify my life and worship, by the Spirit's grace. I pray in Immanuel's name. Amen.

BIBLICAL PERSPECTIVE

At "the beginning of the gospel of Jesus Christ" (Mark 1:1), we encounter the Father, the Son, and the Holy Spirit— three persons acting as one God in Christ's saving mission: "And straightway coming up out of the water, he saw the heavens opened, and the Spirit like a dove descending upon him: and there came a voice from heaven, saying, Thou art my beloved Son, in whom I am well pleased" (Mark 1:10–11).

Christ's commission to the church after His resurrection likewise has a Trinitarian shape: make disciples of all the nations, "baptizing them in the name of the Father, and of the Son, and of the Holy Ghost" (Matt. 28:19). The singular "name" is of the one God, but three persons are listed together here in a parallel structure that gives equal honor to each.

Accordingly, as the apostles brought the gospel to the world, they preached a Trinitarian message of grace. At the opening of Peter's first epistle, he marvels at the Trinitarian work of God in the salvation of Christians by the Father's foreknowledge, the blood of Jesus the Son, and the sanctification of the Holy Spirit unto obedience (1 Peter 1:2). Paul prays to "the Father of our Lord Jesus Christ" for the work of "his Spirit" so that "Christ may dwell in your hearts by faith" (Eph. 3:14–17). John also testified that "the Father sent the Son to be the Saviour of the world," and said that we know God dwells in us "because he hath given us of his Spirit" (1 John 4:13–14).

The Bible's message is clear: God's redemptive work is performed by each of the persons of the Trinity. Although the word *trinity* does not appear in the Bible, the basic doctrine may be summarized in a few short propositions taught in God's Word.

- There is one God.
- The Father is God. The Son is God. The Holy Spirit is God.
- The Father, the Son, and the Holy Spirit are three persons.
- The Father is the Father of the Son. The Son is the Son of the Father. The Spirit is the Spirit of the Father and the Son.
- The Father, the Son, and the Holy Spirit are one God.

Thus, the living God subsists in "three persons…the Father, the Son, and the Holy Ghost; and these three are one God, the same in substance, equal in power and glory."[1] The distinctions among the divine persons do not separate them, but bind them together, for the Father, the Son, and the Holy Spirit indwell each other. Each person of the Trinity completely embraces and encompasses the others in mutual sharing of all divine glory without any person losing His distinct personhood. Let us consider how the Trinity shapes the gospel and our lives.

First, Scripture declares the Trinitarian shape of the gospel. As we saw from 1 Peter 1, each member of the Trinity performs an indispensable function in our salvation. The Father is the initiator of salvation and the sender of the Son and the Spirit. Without God the Father, there would be no one to send the Son and Spirit into the world, to accept

---

1. Westminster Shorter Catechism (Q. 4–6), *Reformed Confessions*, 4:353–54.

the Son's sacrifice, or to hear the Spirit-wrought prayers of the redeemed. Christ did not come of His own accord, but to do the will of the Father (Gal. 1:4). Without the obedience and sufferings of God the Son, no one could escape God's curse or enjoy God's blessing in the Spirit. Likewise, the Spirit directs our hearts toward "Abba, Father." The united work of the Son and the Spirit aims at the Father's glory (Phil. 2:11). Without the renewing work and indwelling presence of God the Spirit, no one would benefit from Christ's redemptive work or have any assurance of being reconciled to God as His child. Apart from the divine Spirit, God could not dwell within the hearts of the redeemed to relate them to the Father and the Son. Without the Trinity, the gospel disappears.

Second, the Trinity is central not only to Christian doctrine, but also to worship and life. The doctrine of the Trinity reminds us that relationships are central to the Christian faith. To worship the triune God in isolation from other Christians is a contradiction in terms. Douglas Kelly says, "God is known in community. This is not least because God is community within Himself."[2] We must not pretend to know the triune God while living in broken relationships with others by failing to do what is in our power to reconcile. Instead, we should strive for peace, harmony, unity, partnership, and deep friendships with God's saints.

The reality of the Trinity also empowers our prayers, inflames our prayers with affection for the triune God, and encourages us to pray unceasingly. The Spirit enables God's

---

2. Douglas F. Kelly, *Systematic Theology: Grounded in Holy Scripture and Understood in the Light of the Church, Volume 1, The God Who Is: The Holy Trinity* (Fearn, Ross-shire, Scotland: Christian Focus, 2008), 555.

adopted sons and daughters to pray to the Father in their deepest sorrows just as the incarnate Son prayed to His Father (Mark 14:36).

Furthermore, if the chief end of man is to glorify God and enjoy Him forever, then it is crucial that we know this God to be the holy Trinity. Do you worship the triune God? Do you adore the Father, the Son, and the Holy Spirit as three persons and one God? Does your faith in the gospel embrace all three persons in the fullness of God's saving economy, or only one or two? Do you find yourself drawn to love the Father and the Spirit when you consider the Son, with the same being true for any of the three persons? The real test of our grasp of the doctrine of the Trinity is not how much we *understand* the true God but how much we *worship* Him.

We should cherish this doctrine, study it in the Holy Scriptures, meditate upon it until it inflames our hearts, and teach and defend it with all the resources of the church.

REFLECTION QUESTIONS

1. How is the gospel Trinitarian? What would happen to the gospel if God were not triune?

2. How does the Old Testament testify to the plurality of persons in God?

3. What are some examples of Trinitarian patterns (Father, Son, Spirit) in the New Testament?

4. What difference does it make to your faith and life that:

  • there is only one God?

  • Jesus Christ is the Son of the Father?

  • Jesus Christ is God?

  • the Holy Spirit is not a force, but your personal Lord?

5. What practical difference should the doctrine of God's Trinitarian nature make in your life?

DIGGING DEEPER

  • Some other Scripture passages about the triune God include John 1:18; 10:38; 14:10–11; 17:21; Romans 8:9; 2 Corinthians 13:14; Galatians 4:4–6; Titus 3:4–6; and 1 John 1:3.

  • Though the Old Testament emphasizes that the Lord is one (Deut. 6:4), we find shadows of the tri-personality of the one God there. The creation account refers to "the Spirit of God" (Gen. 1:2), and Isaiah identifies this Spirit as the Lord of Israel whom the people grieved (Isa. 63:10).

We also encounter the enigmatic figure known as "the angel of the Lord," a person sent by God who nevertheless speaks and acts as the Lord Himself (Gen. 16:7–14; 22:11–18; Ex. 3:1–6; 23:20–22; Num. 22:22, 35, 38; Judg. 2:1–5; 6:11–24; 13:1–22). The Old Testament foretold a divine Messiah. David addressed the coming Christ as "my Lord" and foresaw Him sitting at God's right hand (Ps. 110:1), which can be said of no mere man, but only of God's Son (cf. Matt. 22:41–46; Isa. 9:6; Mic. 5:2; Ps. 45:6–7). Therefore, the King is God, but also stands in a mediatorial relationship with God. With the coming of Jesus Christ, the New Testament brings the doctrine of the Trinity out of the shadows into the full light of day.

• See also John Owen, *Communion with God,* vol. 2 of *The Works of John Owen* (repr., Edinburgh: Banner of Truth, 2014); Ryan McGraw, *Is the Trinity Practical?* (Grand Rapids: Reformation Heritage Books, 2015); Michael Reeves, *Delighting in the Trinity: An Introduction to the Christian Faith* (Downers Grove, Ill.: IVP Academic, 2012); Robert Letham, *The Holy Trinity*, rev. ed. (Phillipsburg, N. J.: P&R, 2019); Fred Sanders, *The Deep Things of God: How the Trinity Changes Everything* (Wheaton, Ill.: Crossway, 2010).

10

GOD IS CREATOR

SCRIPTURE MEDITATION

Who hath measured the waters in the hollow of his hand, and meted out heaven with the span, and comprehended the dust of the earth in a measure, and weighed the mountains in scales, and the hills in a balance?... It is he that sitteth upon the circle of the earth, and the inhabitants thereof are as grasshoppers; that stretcheth out the heavens as a curtain, and spreadeth them out as a tent to dwell in...Lift up your eyes on high, and behold who hath created these things, that bringeth out their host by number: he calleth them all by names by the greatness of his might, for that he is strong in power; not one faileth.... Hast thou not known? hast thou not heard, that the everlasting God, the LORD, the Creator of the ends of the earth, fainteth not, neither is weary? There is no searching of his understanding.

—ISAIAH 40:12, 22, 26, 28

PRAYER

Heavenly Father, Thou hast created me and I am fearfully and wonderfully made. Thou art my Creator and I am Thy creation. Give me a grateful heart that Thou alone art the Creator of the ends of the

earth. Draw me close to Thee, to rest in Thy promises, and to enjoy fellowship with Thee, for Christ's
sake. Amen.

BIBLICAL PERSPECTIVE

"In the beginning God created the heaven and the earth"
(Gen. 1:1). God created all things out of nothing by His
powerful word. God is the only non-created being from all
eternity. The opening chapters of Genesis describe some of
the details surrounding His creative power and the nature
of the creation itself. "And God saw every thing that he had
made, and, behold, it was very good" (Gen. 1:31). There is
nothing evil about God's creation as He created it. It was
declared "good."

The pinnacle of God's creation was man, whom He
created in His own image—male and female (Gen. 1:27).
Being created in the image of God means, first, that man
was created to reflect God's communicable attributes, such
as love, justice, mercy, kindness, goodness, and so forth. But
being created in the image of God also means that man was
created *for relationship*. As we saw in chapter 9, God exists as
one God in three persons: the Father, the Son, and the Holy
Spirit. Therefore, God is, in His essence, relational and has
created us to have a relationship with Him and with others.

That God is Creator means that His creation serves as
an echo and display of His handiwork, power, and wisdom. Creation is God's general revelation to His creatures,
which attests to His eternal power and divine nature (Rom.
1:20). King David exclaims, "The heavens declare the
glory of God; and the firmament sheweth his handywork"
(Ps. 19:1). This characteristic of God as Creator should serve

to bring great humility to our souls as we consider His works. David, again, writes: "When I consider thy heavens, the work of thy fingers, the moon and the stars, which thou hast ordained; what is man, that thou art mindful of him? and the son of man, that thou visitest him?" (Ps. 8:3–4).

We are to give praise to God, for we are fearfully and wonderfully made (Ps. 139:14). Before you were born, God knew all about you (cf. Jer. 1:5), and then you were intricately woven in your mother's womb (Ps. 139:15). God creates all things for His glory, including the birds of the air and the fish of the sea. And He has created *you* for His glory as well and, if you are a true believer, He rejoices over you with gladness (Zeph. 3:17).

It is also important to note that all three persons of the Trinity were involved in creation. As the Spirit hovered over the face of the waters at creation (Gen. 1:2), so also Christ became the agent through whom God created the world. The apostle John writes, "All things were made by [Christ]; and without him was not any thing made that was made" (John 1:3). Likewise, Paul writes, "For by [Christ] were all things created, that are in heaven, and that are in earth, visible and invisible…all things were created by him, and for him" (Col. 1:16). The writer of Hebrews also attests to the involvement of Jesus in creation, "by whom also he made the worlds" (Heb. 1:2).

But man has a propensity toward sin and his heart is an idol factory,[1] bent on turning anything and everything into idols of worship. Paul explains in Romans that humanity

---

1. See John Calvin, *Institutes of the Christian Religion,* ed. John T. McNeill, trans. Ford Lewis Battles (Louisville, Ky.: Westminster John Knox Press, 1960), 1.11.8.

has "changed the glory of the uncorruptible God into an image made like to corruptible man, and to birds, and four-footed beasts, and creeping things" (Rom. 1:23). As sinful men and women, we have turned to worship of the creation rather than worship of the Creator.

But God has sent His only eternal Son to reconcile God's creation to Himself. God's purpose in Christ is to "gather together in one all things in Christ, both which are in heaven, and which are on earth; even in him" (Eph. 1:10). Paul writes "that God was in Christ, reconciling the world unto himself, not imputing their trespasses unto them" (2 Cor. 5:19), that "the creature itself also shall be delivered from the bondage of corruption into the glorious liberty of the children of God" (Rom. 8:21).

Therefore, "if any man be in Christ, he is a new creature: old things are passed away; behold, all things are become new" (2 Cor. 5:17). As God's new creation by faith in Jesus, we have been called to holiness by grace. Because we are saved by God's grace alone, He re-creates us as His "workmanship, created in Christ Jesus unto good works, which God hath before ordained that we should walk in them" (Eph. 2:10). You are God's *workmanship* and His treasured masterpiece. God knows all about you because you are His creation.

From beginning to end, God is declared to be the eternal and wise God, the Creator of the ends of the earth. Not only does He create all things in the universe but also upholds "all things by the word of his power" (Heb. 1:3). It is God who creates, who sustains, and who preserves His people for His glory. By faith in the eternal, *un*created Son—Jesus

Christ—believers are made His new creation to the praise of His glory!

REFLECTION QUESTIONS

1. What do you think Isaiah is trying to communicate by His rhetorical question in Isaiah 40:12? "Who hath measured the waters in the hollow of his hand, and meted out heaven with the span, and comprehended the dust of the earth in a measure, and weighed the mountains in scales, and the hills in a balance?"

2. What other attributes of God come to your mind when you read Isaiah 40:22, "It is he that sitteth upon the circle of the earth, and the inhabitants thereof are as grasshoppers; that stretcheth out the heavens as a curtain, and spreadeth them out as a tent to dwell in"? Why?

3. Isaiah 40:26 tells us that not one star is missing in God's perfect creation. How might that relate to the nature of God's creative work?

4. Take a few minutes to reflect on Isaiah 40:28: "Hast thou not known? hast thou not heard, that the everlasting God, the LORD, the Creator of the ends of the earth, fainteth not, neither is weary?" What are some thoughts that come to your mind?

DIGGING DEEPER

- Some other Scripture passages on God as Creator include Genesis 1–2; Psalms 8; 19:1–6; 139:13–16; 148:5; Ecclesiastes 12:1; Isaiah 42:5; Acts 17:26; Romans 8:19; 2 Corinthians 5:17; Ephesians 2:10, 15; Colossians 1:15–16; 1 Timothy 4:4; Hebrews 1:2; 1 Peter 4:19; and Revelation 10:6.

- God creates both instantly and through secondary means. Instantaneous creation would include salvation. An example of secondary creation would be the growth of a plant. For example, if you plant a seed in good soil and water it, the seed will sprout and grow. You can make a table, but again, the table comes from wood, which comes from a tree, which is from the seed, which God created. God as Creator, then, also means that He is the *source* of all things.

- See also Mark D. Futato, *Creation: A Witness to the Wonder of God* (Phillipsburg, N.J.: P&R, 2000); William Van Doodewaard, *The Quest for the Historical Adam: Genesis, Hermeneutics, and Human Origins* (Grand Rapids: Reformation Heritage Books, 2015).

11

GOD IS SUSTAINER

SCRIPTURE MEDITATION

Cast thy burden upon the LORD, and he shall sustain thee:
he shall never suffer the righteous to be moved.

—PSALM 55:22

PRAYER

Lord God of heaven and earth, even now as I pray to Thee, Thou art sustaining my life—giving me breath and a beating heart. I thank Thee for sustaining my faith and preserving my life by Thy grace. I know that I am safe under Thy watchful care and that Thou art my great Shepherd. Make me to lie down in the green pastures of Thy grace as I meditate on Thee as my Sustainer, for the sake of my worthy and glorious Savior. Amen.

BIBLICAL PERSPECTIVE

To sustain means to uphold, to keep, or to preserve. It means not giving up. God not only creates everything, but *sustains* everything. From the air you are breathing right now to your beating heart, God is keeping you alive for His glory.

God sustains us bodily here on earth until He calls us home to be with Him in heaven. God sustains us spiritually, not letting anyone or anything snatch us out of Christ's sovereign hand (John 10:28). God sustains us emotionally when we just can't bear the pain any longer.

God sustains His whole creation, upholding the universe by the word of His power (Heb. 1:3). In all these ways and more, God is providentially and powerfully working to uphold you, keep you, and preserve you so that you will find joy and hope and respond with a thankful heart.

The apostle Paul writes of the sustaining power of Christ in 1 Corinthians 1:4–9:

> I thank my God always on your behalf, for the grace of God which is given you by Jesus Christ; that in every thing ye are enriched by him, in all utterance, and in all knowledge; even as the testimony of Christ was confirmed in you: so that ye come behind in no gift; waiting for the coming of our Lord Jesus Christ: who shall also confirm you unto the end, that ye may be blameless in the day of our Lord Jesus Christ. God is faithful, by whom ye were called unto the fellowship of his Son Jesus Christ our Lord.

What is amazing about this passage is that Paul links the faithfulness of God to the sustaining power of Christ. God as Sustainer is one aspect of Him being faithful. God sustains our faith, even when we sometimes feel like casting it aside. One way He does this is by continually drawing us into fellowship with Jesus.

Enjoying communion and fellowship with Christ is a means by which God sustains His people. The basis of our communion with Christ is our union with Christ through faith in His saving work. We enter into fellowship through the application of God's Word, through prayer, through the sacraments, through service, and through grace-centered community.

One of the other great truths of Scripture is that, if you are a true believer in Christ, you can never lose your salvation. "Being confident of this very thing, that he which hath begun a good work in you will perform it until the day of Jesus Christ" (Phil. 1:6). While your fellowship with Christ may wax and wane, you will never lose your salvation. However, test your heart to see if you possess true faith. Even mustard-seed faith opens wide the gates of heaven and secures your eternal reward.

Meditate on these words of promise:

> For I the LORD thy God will hold thy right hand, saying unto thee, Fear not; I will help thee. (Isa. 41:13)

> The LORD God is my strength, and he will make my feet like hinds' feet, and he will make me to walk upon mine high places. (Hab. 3:19)

> My grace is sufficient for thee: for my strength is made perfect in weakness. (2 Cor. 12:9)

> He giveth power to the faint; and to them that have no might he increaseth strength. (Isa. 40:29)

That God is Sustainer also dispels fear. A few verses earlier, God says, "Fear thou not, for I am with thee" (Isa. 41:10). The more you rest in the power of God to sustain your life and faith, the more you will be able to fight the fear of man, the fear of death, and the fear of evil.

I mentioned that one of the ways that God sustains us is by His Word. The Bible's message is about Christ crucified and His victory over sin and death for us. God promises believers that "there is therefore now no condemnation to them which are in Christ Jesus" (Rom. 8:1). In other words, God's promises—found in His Word—sustain us. As the psalmist prays: "Uphold me according unto thy word, that I may live" (Ps. 119:116). Rest in the promises of God to sustain your faith, revive your soul, and bring delight to your heart.

REFLECTION QUESTIONS

1. If God is your Sustainer, it should fill you with great hope. But why *hope*?

2. Psalm 55:22 tells us to cast our burden on the Lord. Do you have any burdens that you need to relinquish and cast before the Lord? List some things that you are struggling with at the moment and then meditate on Matthew 11:28–30.

3. How might casting a burden upon the Lord sustain you?

4. If you knew that you were completely safe and secure in Jesus—that you were fully accepted and loved—how might that affect your relationships with people around you?

5. What are some ways that God is sustaining you this very moment—physically, spiritually, or emotionally?

DIGGING DEEPER

- Some other Scripture passages on God as Sustainer include Deuteronomy 7:9; Isaiah 40:29–31; John 10:28; 1 Corinthians 1:4–9; Ephesians 1:14; Philippians 1:6; 2 Timothy 1:8–12; and Hebrews 1:1–3.

- That God *sustains* implies something against which He would need to sustain us. There would be nothing special about sustaining us if there was no *need* to sustain us. In other words, what are we sustained *from*? There is a need for God's sustaining power. We are sinful and cannot sustain ourselves against the attacks of sin, the miseries of this life, and death itself. Can you think of any other reason that we *need* to be sustained?

- See also Burk Parsons, ed., *Assured by God: Living in the Fullness of God's Grace* (Phillipsburg, N.J.: P&R, 2006).

12

GOD IS INFINITE

SCRIPTURE MEDITATION

> *Great is our Lord, and of great power:*
> *his understanding is infinite.*
>
> —PSALM 147:5

PRAYER

All of Thy glorious attributes are infinite, glorious Jehovah, for Thou art infinite. When I consider how great and immeasurable Thou art, I am both humbled and encouraged. Sanctify my heart and mind as I consider the attributes that manifest Thy infinity. Remove from me any ungodly tendency to limit Thee in my thoughts, affections, words, and actions. I pray this in my Master's name. Amen.

BIBLICAL PERSPECTIVE

When we encounter something great and magnificent, we find it both humbling and fascinating. David looked up into the night sky, contemplated the moon and the stars as God's creations, and cried out, "What is man, that thou art mindful of him? And the son of man, that thou visitest him?" (Ps. 8:4). God's glory is "above the heavens" (v. 1), which implies that He is greater than anything we know in this universe.

People use the word infinity to describe God's superlative greatness. God made our minds capable of conceiving His infinity at least by negation: we are finite, but He is not! Hence, Solomon could say, "Will God in very deed dwell with men on the earth? Behold, heaven and the heaven of heavens cannot contain thee; how much less this house which I have built!" (2 Chron. 6:18).

God's infinity speaks of His qualitative transcendence over all conceivable things.[1] We do not mean by infinity that God is utterly indescribable or arbitrary, for He has revealed Himself and always acts consistently according to His very nature.[2] Rather, as Francis Turretin said, God's infinity means that "he embraces every degree of every perfection without any limitation."[3] John Howe said that divine infinity is the "bottomless profundity of essence, and full confluence of all kinds and degrees of perfection, without bound or limit."[4]

Sinners do not love God's infinity for one simple reason: it humbles man. Thomas Watson said, "As the stars disappear at the rising of the sun, oh, how does a man shrink into

---

1. John S. Feinberg, *No One Like Him: The Doctrine of God*, Foundations of Evangelical Theology (Wheaton, Ill.: Crossway, 2001), 245–47.

2. John M. Frame, *The Doctrine of God, A Theology of Lordship* (Phillipsburg, N.J.: P&R, 2002), 544.

3. Francis Turretin, *Institutes of Elenctic Theology*, trans. George Musgrave Giger, ed. James T. Dennison Jr. (Phillipsburg, N.J.: P&R, 1992–1997), 3.8.1, 6 (1:194–95).

4. John Howe, *The Living Temple*, in *The Works of the Rev. John Howe* (London: William Tegg and Co., 1848), 1:98.

nothing when infinite majesty shines forth!"[5] Since the fall of man, people have exchanged the infinite glory of God for finite beings which they worship instead of God. Such "gods" may seem very personal, but they are hardly worthy of worship. Only the God who is infinite in His being and works, and whom sinners can never domesticate, is worthy of our worship.

Comparisons fail us when we consider how great God is: "To whom then will ye liken God? Or what likeness will ye compare unto him?" (Isa. 40:18). All the nations of mankind are to Him but a drop in a bucket or dust on the scales, "less than nothing" in His sight (vv. 15–17). God created the millions of stars in the sky, and each of the celestial lights receives His personal care (v. 26). God never gets tired, His knowledge is limitless, and He will never fail to uphold the cause of His people (vv. 27–28). What a great God! This is the comfort of those who hope in Him, and He grants them strength in their weakness (vv. 29–31).

We should reverently note that the infinity of the triune God is crucial to the gospel. The good news of salvation announces that God's Son "gave himself for us, that he might redeem us from all iniquity" (Titus 2:14). The guilt of our sins against the immeasurably Holy God is enormous (Matt. 18:24). Who could satisfy or repay such a debt for us? Who is this person who gave His life to "redeem us from all iniquity"? He is our glorious "great God and our Saviour Jesus Christ" (Titus 2:13). The person who died on the cross was no less than the infinite God. Though death

5. Thomas Watson, *A Body of Divinity* (Edinburgh: Banner of Truth, 1965), 52.

could have power over His human nature only, the infinite worth of the incarnate Lord imparted infinite value to His atoning work. Therefore, we may rest assured that His blood redeemed innumerable people from all nations (Rev. 7:9, 14)—even the chief of sinners (1 Tim. 1:15). Praise God for the infinite Redeemer!

In the next four chapters, we will meditate upon different aspects of divine infinity. We will consider God's infinity with respect to our understanding (God is incomprehensible), His infinity with respect to His being and well-being (God is self-sufficient), and His infinity with respect to space (God is immense; God is everywhere).

REFLECTION QUESTIONS

1. Think of the different aspects of God's infinity: with respect to time, space, human understanding, and God's well-being. How might this truth be encouraging to weak saints?

2. How does God's attribute of infinity rule out all idolatry and the worship of created things?

3. Why is it crucial that we have an *infinite* God and redeemer?

4. Why might we as sinful human beings dislike or be uncomfortable with the truth of God's infinity?

5. In what ways have you lived your life in denial of certain aspects of God's infinity?

DIGGING DEEPER

- Some other Scripture passages about God's infinity include Exodus 18:11; Job 11:7–10; Psalms 95:3–5; 113:4–6; John 10:29; and Hebrews 6:13.

- The word *infinity* is used of God in the English Bible only in Psalm 147:5: "His understanding is infinite"; literally, "there is no number" (Hebrew *'eyn mispar*), in contrast to "the number [*mispar*] of the stars" (v. 4). The phrase "there is no number" or "without number" can be used hyperbolically of large quantities of people or earthly things, but even there it communicates something beyond ordinary human powers of reckoning.

- Pantheism and panentheism present an impersonal God that manifests personality only in finite avatars of divinity, as in Hinduism. Some people attempt to reformulate biblical religion in terms of a finite God, as in open theism, but the Holy Scriptures reveal the true God to be both infinite and personal, both capable of loving fellowship with mankind and "exalted above all we can know or think," as Charles Hodge wrote.[6]

---

6. Charles Hodge, *Systematic Theology* (1871–1873; repr., Peabody, Mass.: Hendrickson, 1999), 1:380.

- See also Jen Wilkin, *None Like Him: 10 Ways God is Different from Us (and Why That's a Good Thing)* (Wheaton, Ill.: Crossway, 2016); Craig Biehl, *God the Reason: How Infinite Excellence Gives Unbreakable Faith* (Franklin, Tenn.: Carpenter's Son Publishing, 2015).

GOD IS INCOMPREHENSIBLE

13

SCRIPTURE MEDITATION

Canst thou by searching find out God? Canst thou find out the Almighty unto perfection? It is as high as heaven; what canst thou do? deeper than hell; what canst thou know? The measure thereof is longer than the earth, and broader than the sea.

—JOB 11:7–9

PRAYER

Comprehensible yet incomprehensible Lord God, I praise Thee for Thy infinity and incomprehensibility. If man could know Thee fully, Thou wouldst not be God. Thy works are unsearchable, and yet Thou hast sent Thy only begotten Son, and He has made Thee known (John 1:18). Who are we that Thou art mindful of us? Thy mercy is therefore magnified. Bring my mind and heart in submission to the glory of Thy unsearchable being and ways. I pray this in Jesus's name. Amen.

BIBLICAL PERSPECTIVE

God's *incomprehensibility* refers to His infinity with respect to our understanding. We cannot understand God as He understands Himself. His greatness is unsearchable (Ps. 145:3). God's worthiness to be praised goes far beyond anything that we can think or imagine (Eph. 3:20–21). His "glorious name" is "exalted above all blessing and praise" (Neh. 9:5). Calvin said, "How can the human mind measure off the measureless essence of God according to its own little measure?"[1]

Therefore, when we praise God, we must stretch our words beyond their limited meaning to reach toward, though never arriving at, God in His fullness.[2] Like a child trying to touch the sky, we fail, but still point in the right direction. We should seek God, but we should not try to search His depths. Why should we expect to fully comprehend Him? If we did comprehend Him, then He would not be God.[3]

God's incomprehensibility teaches us to submit our minds entirely to God's Word, that we might know the truth about Him. Only the Spirit of God can search the deep things of God, and God has revealed them to us in the words inspired by the Holy Spirit (1 Cor. 2:9–10).

God is incomprehensible not only in the secret depths of His being but also in the open glory of His works. Eliphaz said that God "doeth great things and unsearchable; marvellous things without number" (Job 5:9). Likewise, Job

---

1. Calvin, *Institutes*, 1.13.21.

2. Kelly, *Systematic Theology*, 219.

3. Bavinck, *Reformed Dogmatics*, 2:48.

acknowledged that God "doeth great things past finding out; yea, and wonders without number" (9:10). His works evoke wonder, amazement, and awe.

When the godly see God's unfathomable glory (Job 38:1–4), they repent of their foolish complaints against God when His ways are hard (42:1–6). His glory teaches us to put our hands over our mouths and meekly endure His chastening (40:1–5). Rather than sitting in judgment over God, we learn to sit at His feet, for God alone knows the way of true wisdom, and it begins with the fear of the Lord (28:20–28). Even when God seems far from us and our enemies anticipate our utter ruin, we can praise Him by faith for His incomprehensible righteousness and salvation (Ps. 71:9–15).

Let us learn, then, to glorify the incomprehensible God. We marvel at the stars He created and tremble before the mighty storms He ordains—yet, "Lo, these are [only] parts of his ways: but how little a portion is heard of him? but the thunder of his power who can understand?" (Job 26:14). When our understanding is exhausted, we must learn to admire, for "we can no more search out his infinite perfections, than a man upon the top of the highest mountain can…take a star in his hand."[4] Yet from the mountaintops of biblical truth, we may see and adore God's glory. May God teach us to say with Paul, "O the depth of the riches both of the wisdom and knowledge of God! How unsearchable are his judgments, and his ways past finding out!" (Rom. 11:33).

---

4. Watson, *A Body of Divinity*, 54.

REFLECTION QUESTIONS

1. In what ways is God comprehensible? In what ways is He incomprehensible?

2. Is the fact of God's incomprehensibility a reason not to seek Him? Why or why not?

3. What response did God's incomprehensibility evoke in Job (Job 42:1–6), or in Paul (Rom. 11:33–36)? Accordingly, how should we respond to God's incomprehensibility?

4. How may the incomprehensibility of God's works, in light of the full display of His attributes, be of immense comfort to us when facing the trials of our lives?

5. Think about the following application: "when our understanding is exhausted, we must learn to admire." How does this apply in your current situation?

DIGGING DEEPER

- Some other Scripture passages about God's incomprehensibility include Deuteronomy 29:29; Nehemiah 9:5; Psalms 72:18; 92:5; 139:6, 17–18; 145:3; 147:5; Isaiah 55:8–9; 57:15; Romans 11:33–34; 1 Corinthians 2:10–11; and 1 Timothy 6:13–16.

- A medieval legend held that Augustine, walking along a beach one day while contemplating the Trinity, encountered a boy scooping water out of the sea with a little shell. The boy claimed that he was emptying the sea, which the amused theologian said was impossible to do with a shell. Then he realized how much less he could fit God's infinity into His finite mind.[5]

- T. J. Crawford (1812–1875) said, "The mysteriousness of certain doctrines is not in itself considered any sufficient reason either for excluding them from the articles of the Christian faith, or for discrediting the Christian system on account of them, as unworthy of the divine origin and authority assumed by it."[6] He went on to say, "For surely when we find that God is incomprehensible…we cannot wonder if the doctrines of his inspired word should occasionally have deep things connected with them which

---

5. Joseph Caryl, *An Exposition with Practical Observations upon…the Book of Job* (Berkeley, Mich.: Dust and Ashes; Grand Rapids: Reformation Heritage Books, 2001), 2:249. The story is attributed to a popular compilation of stories about the saints, Jacobus da Varagine, *Legenda Aurea*, The Golden Legend, written in the thirteenth century.

6. T. J. Crawford, *The Mysteries of Christianity: Revealed Truths Expounded and Defended* (repr., Edinburgh: Banner of Truth, 2016), 8.

we cannot fathom, and dark things which we are unable to explore."[7]

- See also Derek Thomas, *Calvin's Teaching on Job: Proclaiming the Incomprehensible God* (Fearn, Ross-shire, Scotland: Christian Focus, 2004); Vern S. Poythress, *Theophany: A Biblical Theology of God's Appearing* (Wheaton, Ill.: Crossway, 2018); K. S. Oliphint, *The Majesty of Mystery: Celebrating the Glory of an Incomprehensible God* (Bellingham, Wash.: Lexham Press, 2016).

---

7. Crawford, *The Mysteries of Christianity*, 9.

14

GOD IS
SELF-SUFFICIENT

SCRIPTURE MEDITATION

*God that made the world and all things therein, seeing that
he is Lord of heaven and earth, dwelleth not in temples made
with hands; neither is worshipped with men's hands, as
though he needed any thing, seeing he giveth to all life, and
breath, and all things.*

—ACTS 17:24–25

PRAYER

Heavenly Father, Thou art dependent upon no one.
From Thee and through Thee and to Thee are all
things. Thou art complete, lacking in nothing. Grant
me, by Thy Spirit, a greater understanding of the
truth that Thou dost not need anything, including
me. I thank Thee that I can be a part of Thy mission
on earth, and I thank Thee that, as I seek faithfully
to plant and water the gospel, Thou dost provide the
growth. Be lifted high in my heart as I consider the
fact that Thou art self-sufficient. I pray this in the
mighty name of Jesus. Amen.

BIBLICAL PERSPECTIVE

When we consider God's infinity with respect to His being and well-being, we realize that God doesn't *need* us. He didn't create the world, the oceans, the tigers, your dog, and people because He was desperately lonely or lacking. He didn't create us to make up for a deficiency in His character or attributes. Rather, God is self-existent and self-sufficient. Theologians call this God's *aseity*.

The living and true God lacks no good thing. He isn't advanced or improved by our existence or efforts. Moreover, God is not dependent upon His creation; rather He is *in*dependent from His creation. Michael Horton writes, "The world is not necessary for God's being or happiness."[1]

Everything exists for the glory of God. He is the Creator and Sustainer of all things. "In him we live, and move, and have our being" (Acts 17:28). Paul writes, "For of him, and through him, and to him, are all things: to whom be glory for ever" (Rom. 11:36). Peter concurs "that God in all things may be glorified through Jesus Christ" (1 Peter 4:11).

Sadly, a quick scan of the American Christian landscape reveals much that is foreign to this. For example, many worship services seem to be more interested in entertainment than truth and more geared toward gimmicks than God. But worship isn't about us. Our salvation isn't "I can do it; God can help." Jesus didn't save you because He has good taste; He saved you for the praise of His own glory.

We can also see the impact of God's self-sufficiency in worship. When we gather in worship each Lord's Day, we

---

1. Michael Horton, *Pilgrim Theology: Core Doctrines for Christian Disciples* (Grand Rapids: Zondervan, 2011), 76.

don't come bringing God something that He doesn't already possess. We are not making up for His perceived neediness. Rather, we come in worship as those who are like sheep— needy, hungry, dependent, and too often wayward.

Worship reveals *our* greatest need, not the Shepherd's. Worship is a reflection of God's own greatness—with faith-filled reverence and joy—in the knowledge of His truth. God is complete in Himself. When we worship Him, we are not adding to His greatness, but rather expressing our satisfaction in *Him* and in *His* greatness.

Our entry into God's creation didn't add to His attributes, but became an occasion, a platform, for the display and expression of His attributes. John Piper writes, "The love of God for sinners is not making much of them, but His graciously freeing and empowering them to enjoy making much of Him."[2]

David Platt has noted that if every local church and ministry organization and denomination were to fall down and blow away, *God would still make a great name for Himself.* We are called into God's mission on earth not because He needs us, but because He loves us. May we recover a God-centered theology that sees Him as complete in Himself and self-sufficient and worship Him as receivers of His sovereign grace.

---

2. John Piper, *God's Passion for His Glory* (Wheaton, Ill.: Crossway, 1998), 34–35.

REFLECTION QUESTIONS

1. Our Scripture passage teaches that God doesn't *need* anything. How does this make you feel?

2. Many of us live with a functional man-centered theology that says: "You can do it; God can help." How is this thinking contrary to God's self-sufficiency?

3. How should the truth of God's self-sufficiency affect our Lord's Day worship?

4. How might the sin of pride hinder your recognition that God is self-sufficient?

5. What is the connection between God's self-sufficiency and God as Creator?

DIGGING DEEPER

- Some other Scripture passages about God's self-sufficiency include Psalm 33:4–12; Isaiah 46:5–11; Ephesians 1:3–11; Hebrews 1:1–3; 1 Peter 1:24–25; and Revelation 22:13.

- The *aseity* (from Latin *a*, "from" and *se*, "self") of God specifically refers to the fact that God is self-existent and, therefore, independent of His creation. As you might recall from our meditation on God's holiness, God's self-sufficiently dovetails with His being *set apart* and distinct from His creation. What other attributes dovetail with God's aseity?

- See also R. C. Sproul, *The Character of God: Discovering the God Who Is* (Ventura, Calif.: Regal, 1995); A. W. Tozer, *The Knowledge of the Holy* (New York: HarperOne, 2009); Joe Thorn, *Experiencing the Trinity: The Grace of God for the People of God* (Wheaton, Ill.: Crossway, 2015).

15

GOD IS IMMENSE

SCRIPTURE MEDITATION

And one cried unto another, and said, Holy, holy, holy, is the LORD of hosts: the whole earth is full of his glory.

—ISAIAH 6:3

PRAYER

O Lord, Thou art immense and infinite—Thy glory is immeasurable. And how often, I confess, are my thoughts of Thee limited by a disproportionate fear of circumstances that Thou rulest over completely—for Thou art not limited by space. As I turn to meditate upon Thy immensity, instill in me a humble heart, confident in Thy covenant presence, and boldness, with strengthened hands, to be about Thy work. I pray this in Immanuel's beautiful name. Amen.

BIBLICAL PERSPECTIVE

God's special presence refers to specific appearances of His glory when He acts to fulfill His covenant through judgment and salvation. Scripture often calls God's special

presence His *countenance* or *face*, and His *dwelling* with us.[1]
Heaven—not the visible skies but the abode of the angels
and the spirits of deceased saints (Heb. 12:22–23)—is the
place in creation where God preeminently dwells to display
His holiness and beauty (Isa. 63:15).[2] The earthly counter-
part to heaven is God's *temple* where He dwells (Jonah 2:7),
which under the gospel is not a physical building but *the
body of His people* (Eph. 2:20–22). In Christ, God dwells in us
by the Holy Spirit's gracious presence and operations (Rom.
8:9; 1 Cor. 6:19–20). When Christ returns, the Lamb that
was slain will be our temple, for the light of God's glory will
radiate from Christ to fill the new creation (Rev. 21:22–23).
Then we will say, "The LORD is there" (Ezek. 48:35). God
will dwell with His people in the new heaven and new earth
without need of any temple, for His presence will be manifested by His glory filling all things (Rev. 21:1–3, 22–23).

When Solomon dedicated the temple, he acknowledged
that God's special presence dwelt in heaven: "But will God
indeed dwell on the earth? Behold, the heaven and heaven
of heavens cannot contain thee; how much less this house
that I have builded?" (1 Kings 8:27; cf. 2 Chron. 2:6). The
special presence of God rests upon His actual presence in all
places. God's *immensity* (literally, "no measure") means that
He cannot be confined to any one place or limited by any
boundary.[3] Thus, "the whole earth is full of his glory" (Isa.
6:3). Stephen Charnock said, "Innumerable worlds cannot

---

1. See, for example, Gen. 32:30; Ex. 25:8; 29:45; 33:11; Deut. 12:11.

2 See Deut. 26:15; 2 Chron. 30:27; Pss. 11:4; 33:13–14; 115:3; Eccl.
5:2; Matt. 6:9; Rev. 4:1–11.

3. Edward Leigh, *A Treatise of Divinity* (London: by E. Griffin for William Lee, 1646), 2:36.

be a sufficient place to contain God; He can only be a sufficient place to Himself."[4]

God's immensity means that He is the Lord of space. Geerhardus Vos said, "He is exalted above all distinction of space, yet at every point in space is present with all His being and as such is the cause of space."[5] Athanasius said, "God is self-existent, enclosing all things, and enclosed by none."[6] As the self-existent One, God is His own home, so to speak. Augustine wrote, "Before God made heaven and earth, before he made the saints, where did he dwell? He dwelt in himself."[7]

Cultivating an awareness of God's immensity will do much to promote godliness in our lives. First, God's immensity *is a great warning against the sins we may choose*. Proverbs 15:3 says, "The eyes of the LORD are in every place, beholding the evil and the good."

Second, the immensity of the Lord *should fill us with the fear of God*. Ezekiel Hopkins (1634–1690) said that we ought to let our conduct "be always as in his sight and under his

---

4. Charnock, *The Existence and Attributes of God*, 1:376.

5. Geerhardus Vos, *Reformed Dogmatics*, trans. and ed. Richard B. Gaffin et al. (Bellingham, Wash.: Lexham Press, 2012–2016), 1:12.

6. Athanasius, *Defence of the Nicene Definition*, 3.11, in *A Select Library of Nicene and Post-Nicene Fathers of the Christian Church, Second Series*, Ed. Philip Schaff and Henry Wace (New York: Christian Literature Co., 1894), 4:157.

7. Augustine, *Enarrationes in Psalmos*, on Ps. 122 [123 ET], 1.4, cited in Peter Lombard, *Sentences*, trans. Giulio Silano (Toronto: Pontifical Institutes of Mediaeval Studies, 2007), 1.37.3 (1:205). See Augustine, *Expositions on the Book of Psalms*, trans. H. M. Wilkins (Oxford: John Henry Parker, 1853), 5:511; and Turretin, *Institutes*, 3.9.5–6 (1:197–98).

eye, with all gravity and seriousness, with all reverence and submission, with all purity and holiness."[8]

Third, God's immensity *encourages us to rely upon Him wholeheartedly*, "for the eyes of the LORD run to and fro throughout the whole earth, to shew himself strong in the behalf of them whose heart is perfect [complete] toward him" (2 Chron. 16:9).

Fourth, God's presence with His people *teaches us to walk with Him*. He calls us to "walk before me" in moral integrity (Gen. 17:1).

Fifth, the immensity of the triune God *can make Christians fearless*. Wherever trials may meet you, hear His promise: "Fear thou not; for I am with thee: be not dismayed; for I am thy God: I will strengthen thee; yea, I will help thee; yea, I will uphold thee with the right hand of my righteousness" (Isa. 41:10).

Sixth, God's immensity *exalts the grace of the triune God*. God the Father dwells in heaven, and yet He also dwells with all His children behind the closed doors of their homes, so that He "seeth in secret" their faithful acts of devotion and will reward them (Matt. 6:1, 4, 6, 9, 18). The Spirit's divine immensity prompts David to exclaim, "Whither shall I go from thy spirit? Or whither shall I flee from thy presence?... If I take the wings of the morning, and dwell in the uttermost parts of the sea; even there shall thy hand lead me, and thy right hand shall hold me" (Ps. 139:7, 9–10). The Son of God revealed that He, too, is the omnipresent deity. Christ promised His church, "For where two or three are

---

8. Ezekiel Hopkins, *On Glorifying God in His Attributes*, in *The Works of the Right Reverend Father in God, Ezekiel Hopkins*, ed. Josiah Pratt (London: by C. Whittingham, for L. B. Seeley et al., 1809), 3:314.

gathered together in my name, there am I in the midst of them" (Matt. 18:20).

If you belong to the people redeemed by the blood of the Lamb, indwelt by the Holy Spirit, and adopted by the Father, then let the truth of God's immensity and omnipresence nurture you in the fear of God and the comfort of the Holy Spirit.

REFLECTION QUESTIONS

1. Meditate on Charnock's comment that no amount of space can contain God, but that only God can "be a sufficient place to Himself." How does this truth glorify God?

2. How should the immensity of God fill you with both the *fear of God* and *fearlessness in life*? How has this been true in your life?

3. How can God's immensity encourage you to rely on Him and walk with Him?

4. Meditate on the immensity of each of the persons of the Trinity. How does the immensity of each contribute to the gospel?

5. What area of challenge in your life, whether of sin or character growth, can the truth of God's immensity help you with?

DIGGING DEEPER

- Some other Scripture passages on God's immensity include Job 34:21–22; Psalms 34:7, 17–22; 62:8; Isaiah 66:1–2; Amos 9:2; Ephesians 2:18; and Hebrews 4:14–16; 10:19–22.

- We may think of God's presence in three ways: essentially—the presence of His full being without spatial limitations; covenantally—the special presence of His self-revealing activity in judgment and salvation; and incarnationally—God joined to human nature in the one Son of God (John 1:14; cf. Isa. 7:14; Matt. 1:23).

- When thinking about God's presence, we can focus upon God's special presence in some places; His essential presence in terms of His transcendence over all locations (immensity); and His presence in all places (omnipresence).

- See also Clarence H. Benson, *Immensity: God's Greatness Seen in Creation* (Chicago: Van Kampen Press, 1937).

16

GOD IS EVERYWHERE

SCRIPTURE MEDITATION

Am I a God at hand, saith the LORD, and not a God afar off? Can any hide himself in secret places that I shall not see him? saith the LORD. Do not I fill heaven and earth? saith the LORD.

—JEREMIAH 23:23–24

PRAYER

Dear omnipresent Lord, I know that Thou art with me even now as I pray. Thou art *Immanuel*—God with us. Thou art my eternal God and Thou art everywhere right now in all of Thy fullness and majesty. Thou fillest all time and space and yet Thou art not bound by time and space. As I turn now to meditate upon Thy character, gently remind me of Thy sovereignty, Thy goodness, and Thy love. Quiet my heart so that I would be still and know that Thou art God, for the sake of Jesus Christ. Amen.

BIBLICAL PERSEPCTIVE

God is an infinite Spirit (John 4:24), who is present everywhere at all times. The universe is full of His divine presence (cf. Isa. 6:3), an attribute called *omnipresence*. He dwells in all of His creation, but is not bound in any way by His creation: "behold, the heaven and heaven of heavens cannot contain thee" (1 Kings 8:27). In addition, wherever He is present, He is *all there* in His fullness. He does not exist more in Atlanta and less in Chicago. He is equally present everywhere.

King David prayed, "Whither shall I go from thy spirit? or whither shall I flee from thy presence?" (Ps. 139:7). We cannot escape the presence of God. For the Christian, this is a sweet and comforting thought; He is with us everywhere. But for the unbeliever, this is a terrible and dreadful reality. The unbeliever cannot hide from the sovereign presence and knowledge of God.

While God is everywhere in His creation, He is nevertheless *distinct* from His creation. In other words, He does not have the same substance as a tree or a rock. His nature and being are altogether distinct and different from the created world. God is both *transcendent* over all His creation (meaning that He is not subject to its confines and limitations) and He is *immanent* in all of His creation (meaning that He is fully present in His creation).

However, God is not equally present *in the same sense* in all His creation. The way in which He is "with" His chosen people, for example, is different from the way He is "with" the unbeliever. Unlike the unbeliever, the Christian is a "temple of the Holy Ghost" (1 Cor. 6:19). God Himself is "in" a believer in a radically different way than He is "in" anything else (cf. John 17:20–26). As Louis Berkhof explains,

"There is an endless variety in the manner in which He is immanent in His creatures."[1]

One of the greatest truths of the gospel is that God is *with* us. Isaiah prophesied of the coming of Jesus when he wrote, "Therefore the Lord himself shall give you a sign; Behold, a virgin shall conceive, and bear a son, and shall call his name Immanuel" (Isa. 7:14; cf. Matt. 1:23). Immanuel, in Hebrew, means "God with us." David acknowledged the God-with-us presence of the Lord, even in the face of suffering: "Yea, though I walk through the valley of the shadow of death, I will fear no evil: for thou art with me" (Ps. 23:4). At Jesus's ascension into heaven, following His resurrection, He told His disciples, "and, lo, I am with you alway, even unto the end of the world" (Matt. 28:20). If you have placed your trust in Jesus Christ alone as your Savior and Lord, He is *with you* right now—savingly, personally, intimately, comprehensively, intercedingly—ever living to make intercession for you (Heb. 7:25).

God is everywhere. But the fullness of His being and character has stepped into the brokenness and misery of this world in the form of a little child. That child grew up and lived a perfect life without sin, to be the unblemished Lamb of God—slain to take away the sins of the world. God is with us in His Son, Jesus. May you be drawn into greater fellowship with God and may your affections be kindled for the God who is everywhere and who is with you. And may God take up residence in your heart as "Christ in you, the hope of glory" (Col. 1:27).

---

1. Louis Berkhof, *Systematic Theology* (Edinburgh: Banner of Truth, 1958), 61.

REFLECTION QUESTIONS

1. In Jeremiah 23:23, God asks a rhetorical question. What do you think the obvious answer is and why is it asked in a rhetorical way—expecting the obvious answer?

2. Do you find it hard to believe sometimes that God is "at hand" and not "far off"?

3. Meditate on the last part of verse 24: "Do not I fill heaven and earth? saith the LORD." What in this statement do you find profound and amazing? Rephrase this statement in your own words.

4. How might the truth that God is everywhere be a terrifying reality to the unbeliever?

5. How might the truth that God is everywhere be a comforting reality to the Christian?

6. Theologically speaking, how is it possible for us, who are sinful, to be *with* God, who is holy? How does the life and death of Jesus relate to this cosmic problem?

DIGGING DEEPER

- Other Scripture passages that speak of God being everywhere include 1 Kings 8:27; Psalms 23:4; 139:7–10; 145:18; Isaiah 66:1; Jeremiah 23:24; Matthew 28:20; John 4:24; Acts 17:27–28; and Hebrews 4:14–16; 12:22–24.

- God's transcendence also bears the understanding that He is a divine Spirit (John 4:24). The *Westminster Shorter Catechism*, Q. 4 asks, "What is God?" Answer: "God is a spirit, infinite, eternal, and unchangeable, in His being, wisdom, power, holiness, justice, goodness, and truth." While He is everywhere, He is above all things because His being is distinct from His creation. He is "high and lifted up" (Isa. 6:1).

- See also D. A. Carson, *The God Who is There: Finding Your Place in God's Story* (Grand Rapids: Baker, 2010); Ann Spangler, *Praying the Names of God: A Daily Guide* (Grand Rapids: Zondervan, 2004); Carol J. Ruvolo, *God With Us: Light From the Gospels* (Phillipsburg, N.J.: P&R, 1998).

GOD IS UNCHANGING

17

SCRIPTURE MEDITATION

Of old hast thou laid the foundation of the earth: and the heavens are the work of thy hands. They shall perish, but thou shalt endure: yea, all of them shall wax old like a garment; as a vesture shalt thou change them, and they shall be changed: but thou art the same, and thy years shall have no end.

—PSALM 102:25–27

PRAYER

Unchangeable Lord, Thou art the great I AM, the unchanging Rock on which my salvation depends. Though I change daily in my attitudes, ambitions, and character, Thou changest not. Thou dost remain constant because Thou art perfect. Guide my meditations and thoughts to the waters of Thy unchanging character. Help me see that Thou art dependable, constant, and true. Grant me grace as I study this attribute to rest in Thy comforting immutability, for Thy dear Son's sake. Amen.

BIBLICAL PERSPECTIVE

God doesn't change. He remains the same—"yesterday, and to day, and for ever" (Heb. 13:8). Christians affirm that God is *immutable*, which means that He is not subject to change in His being, attributes, or will. In other words, God never ceases to be God. He is perfect and He cannot improve or evolve into something greater. It also means that He cannot *de*volve into something lesser.

Because God is eternal (Deut. 33:27; Rev. 1:8), all of His attributes are also eternal. That means that His power is unchanging. His sovereign control never diminishes. His steadfast love never lets go. His holiness remains unshakably pure. He is eternally wise—knowing the end from the beginning. His attributes are unchanging because *God* is unchanging.

James 1:17 states, "Every good gift and every perfect gift is from above, and cometh down from the Father of lights, with whom is no variableness, neither shadow of turning." As the earth revolves around the sun, shadows change because the direction of the light changes. But with God there is no "shadow of turning" because the source, God, doesn't change.

Likewise, God's will, determinations, and decrees do not change. God chose us "before the foundation of the world…according to the good pleasure of his will" (Eph. 1:4–5). God's "eternal purpose" has been realized in Christ Jesus (Eph. 3:11). God doesn't change His mind or think twice about doing something. Because He is all-knowing, all-wise, and all-powerful, He always acts intentionally and perfectly—no more, no less, no exceptions.

As we grow in our knowledge of the character of God, *we* are changed, transformed by the renewing of our minds (Rom. 12:2). R. C. Sproul explains, "When our understanding of God changes, it is not because God has changed. We are the ones who change. God doesn't grow. God doesn't improve with age. God is the Lord everlasting."[1]

God has existed, from eternity past, as one God in three persons. God the Father, God the Son, and God the Holy Spirit are coeternal, of the same nature and divine essence (Heb. 1:1–3). The attributes that may be attributed to the Father are also attributed to the Son and vice versa. Jesus Christ is therefore "the same yesterday, and to day, and for ever" (Heb. 13:8). Jesus manifested the fullness of God (Col. 2:9), and is therefore just as sovereign, powerful, and eternal as the Father and the Holy Spirit. Indeed, the very name that God decided to call Himself—I AM THAT I AM (Ex. 3:14)—reflects the absolute immutability of God's nature.

As jobs come and go, as relationships grow and dwindle, and as our faith changes from weak to strong, you can rest in the truth of God's immutability. He doesn't change. "The LORD is my rock, and my fortress" (Ps. 18:2). He doesn't waver in His promises, falter in His love, or lack confidence in His plans for you. As the psalmist expressed, "He that dwelleth in the secret place of the most High shall abide under the shadow of the Almighty" (Ps. 91:1). The "shadow" of God will never move. You can find rest and assurance in the shelter of the Most High because it is a shelter that will never crumble or fail.

1. R. C. Sproul, *The Character of God: Discovering the God Who Is* (Ventura, Calif.: Regal, 1995), 84.

REFLECTION QUESTIONS

1. In our passage, the psalmist links God's creation to His immutability. How do you think these two things are related?

2. In verse 27, the psalmist relates God's immutability with His years having "no end." What is the relationship between these two?

3. How might knowing that God is immutable bring you comfort?

4. How might knowing that God is immutable affect your prayer life?

5. Could you *trust* a God who constantly changed, grew in knowledge, or evolved into something greater? Why not?

6. If God's purpose, decrees, and will are eternal and unchanging, was Jesus's death on the cross "Plan B"? Read Isaiah 53:10 and Acts 2:22–24.

DIGGING DEEPER

- Some other Scripture passages on the immutability of God include Numbers 23:19–20; Deuteronomy 32:4; 1 Samuel 15:29; Psalms 33:11; 93:2; Jeremiah 31:3; Malachi 3:6; John 13:1; Romans 11:29; Ephesians 1:4–10; 3:11; Hebrews 6:17; James 1:17; and Revelation 1:8.

- Skeptics point to passages in the Bible that speak of God changing His mind or repenting (cf. Gen. 6:6; Ex. 32:14). However, many other passages are clear that He *doesn't* change His mind (cf. Num. 23:19; 1 Sam. 15:29; Ps. 33:11; Heb. 6:17). There are many places in Scripture where the writers used what has been called "phenomenological language"—which describes events as they *appear* to the observer (for example, God's "hand," "eyes," "waking up," etc.). God "changing His mind" is how it appeared to Moses's finite and limited knowledge.

- Another question people often ask is, "If Jesus is God and Jesus died, did God die?" The answer is that Jesus was truly God and truly man. His *human* nature died, while His *divine* nature can never die or change (cf. Heb. 13:8). We call this God's *impassibility* (not able to suffer or die). Likewise, Scripture teaches that Jesus increased in wisdom and in years (Luke 2:52). In His human nature, Jesus grew in wisdom and had birthdays, like you and me. But He was fully God *and* fully man.

- See also Philip Graham Ryken, *Discovering God in Stories from the Bible* (Phillipsburg, N.J.: P&R, 2010); A. W. Pink, *The Attributes of God* (Grand Rapids: Baker, 1975).

18 GOD IS ALL-KNOWING

SCRIPTURE MEDITATION

O LORD, thou hast searched me, and known me. Thou knowest my downsitting and mine uprising, thou understandest my thought afar off. Thou compassest my path and my lying down, and art acquainted with all my ways. For there is not a word in my tongue, but, lo, O LORD, thou knowest it altogether. Thou hast beset me behind and before, and laid thine hand upon me. Such knowledge is too wonderful for me; it is high, I cannot attain unto it.

—PSALM 139:1–6

PRAYER

All-knowing, heavenly Lord, I echo the prayer of this psalm. I come to Thee telling Thee everything about me as if Thou knowest nothing about me, yet knowing that Thou knowest everything about me. Thou knowest all that I am, and all that I have thought, said, and done, and all that I will think, say, and do. I praise Thee because Thou art all-knowing and yet hast not destroyed me but hast had mercy upon me through Thy Almighty Son. I thank Thee for Thy amazing grace from the bottom of my heart. I thank Thee too that Thou hast ordained every detail of my life, and indeed, all things according to Thy wise, powerful, and intimate knowledge of Thy creation. As I take this time to meditate upon Thy Word and upon Thy infinite and intimate knowledge, fill me with greater humility and greater love for Thee, for the sake and glory of Him whose name is wonderful Counselor, mighty God, and everlasting Father. Amen.

BIBLICAL PERSPECTIVE

God is *omniscient*, which means that He is all-knowing. There is not one thought, one word, or one deed that dodges the knowledge of God. God knows all past events, present events, and future events. And He doesn't just know *about* them. He knows their every detail because His knowledge is tied to Him being the sovereign Creator.

God knows all that happens because He is in control of all that happens (Isa. 46:8–11). However, as we will see later in our meditation on His sovereignty, this control doesn't make us mere robots. We have responsibility under the sovereign control and power of God. But He knows our thoughts even before we think them. He knows our actions before we lift a finger. "But the very hairs of your head are all numbered" (Matt. 10:30). He knew that you would be reading this right now. God knows all that will happen because the future is completely dependent upon His sovereign will and purpose (Eph. 1:7–10).

His knowledge is also tied to the fact that He has created all things. Because He is the Author of life and Creator of the universe, He is perfectly acquainted with His creation.

All things were created by Him and for His glory. That is why you were created—to glorify Him and to enjoy Him forever.[1] As a potter is well acquainted with his clay, so also God is well acquainted with His creation (Rom. 9:20–23).

God knew that Adam would sin in the Garden of Eden and He knew that His only Son would suffer and die for His bride (Eph. 5:25). As Luke writes, "Him, being delivered by the determinate counsel and foreknowledge of God, ye have taken, and by wicked hands have crucified and slain" (Acts 2:23). In God's eternal knowledge, Jesus was slain—as it were—from before "the foundation of the world" (Rev. 13:8).

Jesus, as the full embodiment of God, also knew all things. After Jesus's resurrection from the dead, Peter proclaims to Him, "Lord, thou knowest all things" (John 21:17). As the "wisdom of God" (1 Cor. 1:24), Jesus becomes *our* wisdom by faith in His life, death, and resurrection for salvation (1 Cor. 1:30). Paul writes that in Christ "are hid all the treasures of wisdom and knowledge" (Col. 2:3).

The Bible also speaks of God knowing His elect intimately, which is called "*fore*knowledge." It should be clear that God does not merely look down the corridor of time and know who will believe in Him. While that is certainly true—and is part of His omniscience—He knows who will believe because He has predestined them to believe. Again, the apostle Paul explains: "For whom he did foreknow, he *also* did predestinate to be conformed to the image of his Son" (Rom. 8:29, emphasis mine). Peter writes that

---

1. This is the answer to the Westminster Shorter Catechism's Question 1: "What is the chief end of man?"

believers are "elect according to the foreknowledge of God the Father" (1 Peter 1:2). Paul teaches in 1 Corinthians 8:3, "If any man love God, the same is known of him," and in 2 Timothy 2:19, "The Lord knoweth them that are his."

God's knowledge of His people, the children of God, is saving, intimate, and comprehensive. God tells Jeremiah, "Before I formed thee in the belly I knew thee" (Jer. 1:5). Conversely, Jesus tells certain people who were pretending to be Christians, "I never knew you: depart from me, ye that work iniquity" (Matt. 7:23). Jesus is the Good Shepherd, who said, "I...know my sheep, and am known of mine" (John 10:14).

Indeed, God knows everything. Nothing happens outside the knowledge of God. As the Old Testament writers looked ahead to the coming Messiah, the Lord Jesus Christ, they were carried along by the Holy Spirit (2 Peter 1:21), who had complete and perfect knowledge of all the details surrounding the coming of Christ. These prophecies could only be given by One who was all-knowing.

May we join the heavenly chorus in praise of God as we echo back to Him the truth of His Word: "O the depth of the riches both of the wisdom and knowledge of God!" (Rom. 11:33). Would we strive to know Christ (Phil. 3:10), and may our love "abound yet more and more in knowledge" (Phil. 1:9). May you "grow in grace, and in the knowledge of our Lord and Saviour Jesus Christ. To him be glory both now and for ever. Amen" (2 Peter 3:18).

REFLECTION QUESTIONS

1. As you reflect now on Psalm 139:1–6, can you think of any secret sin you might have thought God didn't know about?

2. King David knew His God and His God knew him. He was a man after God's own heart (1 Sam. 13:14). In what ways can you praise God for knowing you intimately?

3. How might God's full knowledge of you—your sins, your struggles, your gifts, and your weaknesses—fill you with both fear and comfort?

4. In verse 2, David prays, "Thou understandest my thought afar off." Discernment leads to a knowledge of both the content of your thoughts and the motives behind them. How have your thoughts been lately? Have you tried "bringing into captivity every thought to the obedience of Christ" (2 Cor. 10:5)?

5. In verse 6, David expresses that he "cannot attain" the "high" knowledge of God. Yet this was the temptation of Satan to Adam and Eve in the Garden of Eden (Gen. 3:5)—to attain the knowledge of God. How might you (in subtle ways) have boasted or have been prideful of your own knowledge before others—while not acknowledging how limited your knowledge really is, especially when compared to the knowledge of God? Take a few moments to search your heart and repent of this pride in specific areas.

DIGGING DEEPER

- Some other Scripture passages on God's omniscience include Job 23:10; Psalm 90:8; 103:14; 139:23–24; 147:5; Proverbs 19:21; Isaiah 46:8–11; Jeremiah 1:5; Ezekiel 11:5; Daniel 2:22; Hosea 7:2; Amos 3:2; John 21:17; Acts 2:23; 15:18; Romans 8:29–30; 11:33–36 and 1 Peter 1:2.

- If God didn't know all things, could He make any promises? Could you trust Him? The absolute and perfect knowledge of God should be a core belief, and yet it is one we do not ponder enough. Try to make your meditations on God's knowledge applicable to where you are in your life right now.

- See also John M. Frame, *The Doctrine of the Knowledge of God* (Phillipsburg, N.J.: P&R, 1987); Edward A. Dowey, *The Knowledge of God in Calvin's Theology* (Grand Rapids: Eerdmans, 1994).

19 GOD'S FOREKNOWLEDGE

SCRIPTURE MEDITATION

Remember the former things of old: for I am God, and there is none else; I am God, and there is none like me, declaring the end from the beginning, and from ancient times the things that are not yet done, saying, My counsel shall stand, and I will do all my pleasure.

—ISAIAH 46:9–10

PRAYER

Our Father which art in heaven, I praise and worship Thee because by Thy foreknowledge Thou dost direct the whole universe—from the greatest events in history to the minute details of my daily life. Because Thou art good, I can be confident in the wisdom of all things that Thou dost ordain. As I contemplate Thy foreknowledge, grant me a heart of awe, worship, humility, and hope. I pray this for Jesus's sake, with the pardoning of all my sins in His precious blood. Amen.

BIBLICAL PERSPECTIVE

Throughout the Bible, God reveals future events before they take place, and His word proves true. The Lord says, "I am God, and there is none like me, declaring the end from the beginning" (Isa. 46:9–10). God's omniscience of the future is called His "foreknowledge"—and this attribute distinguishes Him from all other beings.

God demonstrated His foreknowledge in His covenantal dealings with Abraham (Gen. 12:3; 15:13; Gal. 3:8), Joseph (Genesis 37, 40–41), and Moses (Ex. 3:19–20; 4:21–23). God's foreknowledge is so reliable that He made it a test of a true prophet, saying through Moses, "When a prophet speaketh in the name of the LORD, if the thing follow not, nor come to pass, that is the thing which the LORD hath not spoken, but the prophet hath spoken it presumptuously: thou shalt not be afraid of him" (Deut. 18:22).

Isaiah's prophecies against false gods stand upon the divine ability to declare the future: "Let them bring them forth, and shew us what shall happen: let them shew the former things, what they be, that we may consider them, and know the latter end of them; or declare us things for to come. Shew the things that are to come hereafter, that we may know that ye are gods" (Isa. 41:22–23). God is not ignorant of the future in any respect, or He would not be God. His divine nature guarantees that He has exhaustive knowledge of all things from all eternity.

The greatest event of history that fulfilled predictive prophecy was the advent and work of God's Son—the great theme of the Old Testament (Luke 24:44–47). The prophets foretold that Christ would be of the tribe of Judah (Gen. 49:10) and from the family of David (Isa. 9:6–7). He would be born of a virgin (Isa. 7:14) in the town of Bethlehem (Mic. 5:2), but would bring the light of God to Galilee (Isa. 9:1–2). He would be a prophet like Moses, declaring God's word and working miracles (Deut. 18:15–19; 34:10–12). Another preacher would go ahead of Him, calling Israel to prepare itself for the coming of the Lord (Isa. 40:3; Mal. 3:1). Christ would be rejected by the leaders of the nation, but God would make Him the foundation of His new temple (Ps. 118:22–26). He would ride into Jerusalem as a king humbly riding on a donkey (Zech. 9:9). His sorrows would overwhelm Him as His enemies pierced His hands and feet, and mocked Him as He died, and as God Himself abandoned Him to judgment (Ps. 22:1, 7, 13, 16). He would meekly bear the sins of His people and suffer the punishment they deserved, yet He would be buried in the place of the rich (Isa. 53:5–9). God would raise Him from the dead (Ps. 16:10–11) and exalt Him to sit at His right hand in supreme glory (110:1). Subsequently, He would send out the good news so that people from all nations would become worshipers of God (22:22, 27).

The way God has demonstrated His foreknowledge in all the fulfilled prophecies of His Son should fuel joy and adoration among us. God's infallible foreknowledge of all future events has rich applications to the Christian life. We should respond to this biblical truth with awe, worship, humility, and hope.

First, we should cultivate *awe* by never growing so familiar with the doctrine of foreknowledge that we fail to be astonished that God knows the future before it exists. Who is God, that He knows the end from the beginning? A. W. Pink said, "How far exalted above the wisest man is the

Lord! None of us knows what a day may bring forth, but all futurity is open to his omniscient gaze."[1]

Second, we ought to *praise* and *worship* the Lord as the God of the future, and thus the only true God. We are to glorify Him, for He alone among all beings is able to know the future with certainty. False gods do not know what will come; in fact, they know nothing at all. Men are often surprised and left scrambling to adjust their plans. The God of Israel is the Lord of the future, and He alone is worthy of our worship.[2]

Third, we should cultivate *humility* by acknowledging that He is Lord of the future, and we are not. We must make our plans meekly, for we "know not what shall be on the morrow." We ought to say instead, "If the Lord will, we shall live, and do this, or that" (James 4:14–15). God's foreknowledge of the future reminds us that we are not God and our times are in His hands (Ps. 31:15). Let us therefore not lean on our own intelligence, but trust in the Lord and commit our plans to Him (Prov. 3:5–6; 16:3).

Fourth, we must cultivate *hope* by trusting God's promises for the future. Not one of His words of salvation and judgment can fall to the ground (1 Sam. 3:19; 2 Kings 10:10). We should especially trust that great promise that the Lord Jesus Christ will return in divine glory to judge the earth and bring everlasting joy to His people. Nothing can derail God's plan to glorify Himself in Christ. He says to us,

---

1. Pink, *The Attributes of God*, 25–26.

2. Ussher, *A Body of Divinity: Being the Sum and Substance of the Christian Religion*, intro. Crawford Gribben (Birmingham, Ala.: Solid Ground, 2007), 2nd head (38).

"These words are true and faithful" (Rev. 21:5). Let us stake our lives on them and lift up our heads in all our trials.

REFLECTION QUESTIONS

1. What are some Scripture passages that show that God foreknows our future free decisions?

2. How did Christ demonstrate His foreknowledge of the future at the Last Supper?

3. Meditate on the doctrine that God knew your whole life before you were born. How does this truth affect you? How can you use it to cultivate amazement, worship, humility, and hope?

4. Think about A. W. Pink's comment that "None of us knows what a day may bring forth, but all futurity is open to his omniscient gaze." How does this apply to your current situation?

5. Of the four applications mentioned above—awe, worship, humility, and hope—which one is the least developed in you and most in need of improvement?

DIGGING DEEPER

- Some other Scripture passages on God's foreknowledge include Psalm 139:4; Jeremiah 1:5; 29:11; Acts 15:18; Romans 8:29; 1 Corinthians 15:3–4; and 1 Peter 1:2, 20.

- Foreknowledge does not mean that our choice is not involved in our actions. Augustine said that God's foreknowledge of our actions does not break the link between what we do and why we do it. Our choices cause our actions. We do not deny the reality of the human will, but we subordinate it to God's infinitely greater will.[3]

- How does God know the future? Does His knowledge cause it to take place? God eternally knows all that will take place in history because He decreed it before time began, and He will execute His decree through His unfailing providence. He declares the end from the beginning (Isa. 46:9–10). The Lord knows the future because He knows His will. This is *decretal foreknowledge*.

- Christ's own display of foreknowledge reveals His divine nature as God the Son. The Lord Jesus predicted His rejection, death, and resurrection (Luke 9:22); the mar-

---

3. Augustine, *The City of God*, 5.9, in *A Select Library of Nicene and Post-Nicene Fathers of the Christian Church*, ed. Philip Schaff (New York: Christian Literature, 1888), 2:91–92.

tyrdom of Peter (John 21:18–19); and the destruction of Jerusalem (Luke 21:20–24). Christ told His disciples that one of them would betray Him, whom He identified discreetly as Judas (John 13:21–26). Christ said, "Now I tell you before it come, that, when it is come to pass, ye may believe that I am he" (v. 19), literally, "I am" (*eg eimi*). The Lord Jesus used His foretelling of the future to reveal that He is the same Lord who told Moses "I AM" (Ex. 3:14), and who said through Isaiah, "I the LORD, the first, and with the last; I am he" (Isa. 41:4; cf. 43:10, 13; 48:12).

• See also Thomas R. Schreiner and Bruce A. Ware, *Still Sovereign: Contemporary Perspectives on Election, Foreknowledge and Grace* (Grand Rapids: Baker, 2000); Sam Storms, *Chosen for Life: The Case for Divine Election* (Wheaton, Ill.: Crossway Books, 2007).

GOD IS WISE

20

SCRIPTURE MEDITATION

O the depth of the riches both of the wisdom and knowledge of God! how unsearchable are his judgments, and his ways past finding out! For who hath known the mind of the Lord? or who hath been his counsellor? Or who hath first given to him, and it shall be recompensed unto him again? For of him, and through him, and to him, are all things: to whom be glory for ever. Amen.

—ROMANS 11:33–36

PRAYER

Gracious God, how often I succumb to thinking, in subtle ways, that I know more than Thee. I think that I know what's best for me and others and that my view is right. Please break me of this pride so that I may recognize Thee as infinitely wise, all knowing, and all powerful. Thou dost know what is good, true, and right, and Thou dost guide my steps. Wouldst Thou give me the humility and strength to lean not upon my own understanding, but continually look unto Thee for wisdom and guidance? I pray this in the name of my wise King and Lord, Jesus Christ. Amen.

BIBLICAL PERSPECTIVE

Biblical wisdom is right knowledge displayed rightly. That God is wise means that He perfectly displays perfect knowledge in His Word, in creation, in providence, and in redemption. Wisdom combines knowledge with righteousness. It has a moral quality to it in that it is—in its essence—good, true, and noble.

Wisdom is different from mere knowledge. A person can be very knowledgeable about something, but lack wisdom. For example, you can know all there is to know about calculus or the biology of a frog, but that doesn't mean that you know how to use that knowledge *rightly* in everyday life. Human wisdom, therefore, is right knowledge displayed rightly, under the fear of the Lord, for the love of God and love of neighbor.

Ascribing wisdom to God is essentially placing your trust in His knowledge, power, and goodness. When we say that God is perfectly wise, we are saying that—according to His infinite knowledge—He always acts with the best perspective and the best means to display His glory. We trust in His plan for our lives because He is all-knowing, all-powerful, and good. As Proverbs 3:5–6 states: "Trust in the LORD with all thine heart; and lean not unto thine own understanding. In all thy ways acknowledge him, and he shall direct thy paths."

The wisdom literature of the Old Testament includes the books of Job, Psalms, Proverbs, Ecclesiastes, and Song of Solomon. In each of these, two clearly defined ways of living are presented: the way of the wise and the way of the fool. The wise keep the fear of the Lord before them and acknowledge Him in every aspect of life. The fool, on the other hand, shuns the character of God and seeks to live life independently of God (much like Adam and Eve did in the garden).

Proverbs 9:10 states, "The fear of the Lord is the beginning of wisdom: and the knowledge of the holy is understanding." Fearing God means having a reverence and awe before Him—in view of His holiness, glory, power, and might. Pride vanishes from the heart when a healthy fear of God comes in. But fearing God is the *beginning* of wisdom. It's the starting point and foundation of wisdom. True wisdom, then, has a God-centered approach to living—in every area of life. From school to work, from family to friends, being wise must start with a right knowledge and fear of God.

The more we align our thoughts and hearts with the thoughts of God found in His Word, the more we will appropriate and display godly wisdom because wisdom comes from God. James writes, "If any of you lack wisdom, let him ask of God, that giveth to all men liberally, and upbraideth not" (James 1:5). It is easy to get tunnel vision, especially in the midst of suffering. But godly wisdom sees day-to-day struggles from a heavenly perspective and lifts hearts to trust in the God who is infinitely wise, powerful, and good.

In addition, Paul teaches that God's wisdom is "manifold" (Eph. 3:10). It is interesting that in the Greek version of the Old Testament[1] the word used to describe Joseph's coat of many colors (Gen. 37:3) is the same word used in Ephesians 3:10 to talk of God's "manifold" wisdom. In

---

1. Called the Septuagint (LXX). This was a translation of the Hebrew Scriptures completed in 132 BC.

other words, God's wisdom is like a multicolored tapestry, woven together in a beautiful display of mystery, goodness, grace, and truth.

It should also be noted that godly wisdom and worldly wisdom are oftentimes opposites. Paul writes in 1 Corinthians 1:21, "For after that in the wisdom of God the world by wisdom knew not God, it pleased God by the foolishness of preaching to save them that believe." Worldly wisdom cannot "find" God. A person cannot save himself by worldly wisdom—salvation must come by grace alone. The gospel is *foolishness* in the eyes of the world. We die to live and give to gain. Jesus wore a crown of thorns, not gold.

Finally, the wisdom of God is fully displayed in the person of Jesus Christ (1 Cor. 1:24), whom God has made *our* wisdom. Paul explains: "But of him are ye in Christ Jesus, who of God is made unto us wisdom, and righteousness, and sanctification, and redemption" (1 Cor. 1:30). By faith in Christ, He becomes our wisdom so that we now have the ability and freedom to know God as Father and His Son Jesus as Savior and Lord.

REFLECTION QUESTIONS

1. In Romans, Paul unpacks the gospel message and the glorious grace of God in a salvation that is received by faith alone in the finished work of Christ alone. Here in Romans 11:33–36, Paul's language explodes into a chorus of praise. Theology erupts into doxology. How might meditating on the wisdom of God set your heart to praise Him?

2. What do you think Paul is communicating when he says that God's judgments are "unsearchable" in the context of Romans 11:33–36?

3. Do you know anyone who you might consider "wise"? Why would you say that he or she is wise? How might that characteristic reflect God's wisdom?

4. Romans 11:36 says, "For of him, and through him, and to him, are all things." How might this truth relate to the wisdom of God?

5. Moses prays in Psalm 90:12, "So teach us to number our days, that we may apply our hearts unto wisdom." How might studying God's Word teach us about seeing our lives from an eternal perspective, so that we might get a "heart of wisdom"?

6. Do you have any important decisions coming up? Do you need wisdom? Take some time to ask God to grant you wisdom in making the right decision.

DIGGING DEEPER

- Some other Scripture passages on the wisdom of God include 1 Kings 4:29; Psalm 111:10; Proverbs 1:7; 9:10; Daniel 2:20; 1 Corinthians 1:18–31; Ephesians 3:10; and James 1:5; 3:17.

- In the Bible, the words translated as "wisdom" (Hebrew *khakmah*, Greek *sophia*) carry the nuance of practical skill, such as in artistic craftsmanship (Ex. 28:3; 31:3–6; 35:31–35; 1 Kings 7:14; 1 Chron. 28:21). The Lord exhibited His skill in the creation of the world. The psalmist said, "O LORD, how manifold are thy works! In wisdom hast thou made them all: the earth is full of thy riches" (Ps. 104:24; cf. 136:5). God's wisdom gives the universe its structure and stability (Prov. 3:19), so that wise men and women can study it (1 Kings 4:29–34), and we rely upon its law-like behavior (cf. Jer. 33:20, 25). God wisely set the sun and earth at just the right distance from each other: closer and we would fry, but farther away and we would freeze.[2] The infinite wisdom of the Creator distinguishes Him from the false gods worshiped by this world (10:11–12).

• See also Warren W. Wiersbe, *Be Wise: Discern the Difference Between Man's Knowledge and God's Wisdom* (Colorado Springs, Colo.: David Cook, 2010); J. I. Packer, *Knowing God* (Downers Grove, Ill.: InterVarsity Press, 1993).

---

2. Watson, *A Body of Divinity*, 72.

21

GOD IS SOVEREIGN

SCRIPTURE MEDITATION

Hearken unto me, O house of Jacob, and all the remnant of the house of Israel, which are borne by me from the belly, which are carried from the womb: and even to your old age I am he; and even to hoar hairs will I carry you: I have made, and I will bear; even I will carry, and will deliver you. To whom will ye liken me, and make me equal, and compare me, that we may be like?... Remember this, and shew yourselves men: bring it again to mind, O ye transgressors. Remember the former things of old: for I am God, and there is none else; I am God, and there is none like me, declaring the end from the beginning, and from ancient times the things that are not yet done, saying, My counsel shall stand, and I will do all my pleasure: calling a ravenous bird from the east, the man that executeth my counsel from a far country: yea, I have spoken it, I will also bring it to pass; I have purposed it, I will also do it.

—ISAIAH 46:3–5, 8–11

PRAYER

Sovereign, triune King of kings, nothing is outside of Thy absolute control and power. I praise Thee that Thou dost uphold the universe by the word of Thy power and that nothing can thwart Thy plans. Now, as I enter into this meditation on Thy sovereignty, please soften my heart and make me teachable to understand more of Thy character, so that I may have greater faith and delight in Thee and in Thy plans for my life. I pray this in the strong name of Jesus Christ the Lord. Amen.

BIBLICAL PERSPECTIVE

That God is sovereign means that He is in absolute control over all things. Not the tiniest molecule, the fiercest tornado, or the wisest thought is outside the control of God. He does what pleases Him and nothing and no one can throw a wrench in His divine plan. From Adam's fall in the Garden of Eden (Genesis 2), to the death of Christ on the cross (Acts 2:23), to the coming of Christ at the last judgment (1 Thess. 4:15–17), all actions and events that take place, happen under the sovereign hand of God.

Practically speaking, God's sovereignty is displayed in both His *eternal decrees* and His day-to-day *providences*. His eternal decrees include His electing love, which has predestined—from before the foundation of the world— those who would believe in Him (Eph. 1:4–6; Rom. 8:29). In other words, God has graciously chosen a people from before time began to be *His* people—loved and cherished (1 Thess. 1:4). These decrees also include all of His promises made throughout Scripture. If God were not in complete control, He could not promise anything and be able to follow through with those promises. In fact, we could not trust God at all because something else could thwart His promises. But there is nothing that is outside of God's governing power, wisdom, and control.

The other way that we see God's sovereignty displayed is in His providence. God's providence, as the *Westminster Shorter Catechism* (Q. 11) explains, is "his most holy, wise, and powerful preserving and governing all his creatures, and all their actions." Proverbs 16:33 states: "The lot is cast into the lap; but the whole disposing thereof is of the LORD." Providence refers to the expression and action of God's sovereignty. As light shines from the sun, so providence shines from God's sovereignty. They go hand in hand.

At first, this attribute of God's sovereignty might cause you to shrink in self-defense: "If God is really this powerful and has this much control, doesn't that just make me a robot, with no real choice or freedom?" But J. I. Packer writes, "That God's rational creatures, angelic and human, have free agency (power of personal decision as to what they shall do) is clear in Scripture throughout."[1] In other words, while God is absolutely sovereign over all things, we do have certain abilities and choices. God is sovereign; man is responsible.

Unbelievers, to be clear, do not have free moral choice. Before receiving salvation in Christ, all of humanity is dead in sin (Eph. 2:1), unable to even long for God apart from His initiating grace (John 3:3; 6:44; Rom. 8:7). But when God's grace breaks into the sinner's heart, he or she receives a new heart (Ezek. 36:26), one that responds with faith, love, and freedom. God is sovereign; man is responsible. Both hold

---

1. J. I. Packer, *Concise Theology: A Guide to Historic Christian Beliefs* (Carol Stream, Ill.: Tyndale House Publishers, 1993), 33.

together in a mysterious harmony. "A man's heart deviseth his way: but the LORD directeth his steps" (Prov. 16:9).

It is beyond the scope of this brief meditation to explore the relationship between God's sovereignty and human suffering, but suffice it to say that God is in control of all things, including human suffering. There are many reasons why God would allow suffering, from sharing in the sufferings of Christ (Phil. 3:10), to bringing glory to God (John 21:19), to savoring *Him* as the all-satisfying Savior that He is (Ps. 73:25–26), rather than the fleeting pleasures of this earthly life. In any case, it is important to remember that you and I are on an earthly pilgrimage to a heavenly home.

Even the death of God's own Son was part of "Plan A." When Peter preached at Pentecost in Acts 2, he boldly proclaimed that Jesus, "being delivered by the determinate counsel and foreknowledge of God, ye have taken, and by wicked hands have crucified and slain" (v. 23). The Old Testament prophet Isaiah looked ahead to the suffering Christ and wrote that "it pleased the LORD to bruise him" (Isa. 53:10). The Son was crushed for you. The Son was forsaken on your behalf. The Son experienced hell so that you would never have to. Indeed, "with his stripes we are healed" (v. 5).

If Jesus Christ is your Savior and Lord, God promises His providential and loving care: "And we know that all things work together for good to them that love God, to them who are the called according to his purpose" (Rom. 8:28). God's sovereignty should be a source of great comfort to your soul. You are held by a love unlike anything else in all of creation. You are held by a steadfast love that won't let you go (Rom. 8:39). Moreover, nothing will be able to snatch you out of the hands of your Savior (John 10:28)!

REFLECTION QUESTIONS

1. In Isaiah 46:3–5, God communicates that from birth to gray hairs He will *carry* His people. What do you think He is trying to communicate to them? How might this affect your view of life?

2. In our passage, God talks of listening (v. 3), remembering (v. 8–9), and recalling (v. 8). Take a few moments now to recall God's works in your life—how He has preserved you until now and graciously led you from birth. Why might thinking about these things be a difficult task?

3. What promise do you find in verse 4? "Even to your old age I am he; and even to hoar hairs will I carry you: I have made, and I will bear; even I will carry, and will deliver you."

4. Verse 9 reads, "For I am God, and there is none else." Are there any "gods" or idols in your life right now that are hindering your worship of the true and living God? (Note: you might be worshiping what you are afraid of losing, including reputation, security, money, or people.)

5. Verse 10 tells us that God declares "the end from the beginning, and from ancient times the things that are not yet done." How might this truth comfort your soul, in whatever circumstances you are in right now?

6. If God were not in complete control, could you trust Him to keep any promise? Why or why not?

7. Just before His arrest, Jesus prayed about His impending suffering, "Not my will, but thine, be done" (Luke 22:42). How might this inform how *we* ought to pray?

DIGGING DEEPER

• Other Scripture passages on God's sovereignty include Genesis 12:1–3; 50:20; Exodus 15:18; Psalms 33; 47; 93; 97; 115:3; Proverbs 16; Isaiah 24:23; Daniel 4:34; Matthew 10:29–31; Acts 13:26–39; Ephesians 1:10; and Revelation 1:4–8.

• Take some time and meditate on Philippians 2:12–13, where Paul exhorts the Philippians to "work out your own salvation with fear and trembling. For it is God which worketh in you both to will and to do of his good pleasure." In this, man is responsible and is given a command. Yet, God remains sovereign as the One who works in us for His good pleasure.

• See also A. W. Pink, *The Sovereignty of God* (Edinburgh: Banner of Truth, 2009).

22

GOD IS OMNIPOTENT

SCRIPTURE MEDITATION

Ah Lord GOD! behold, thou hast made the heaven and the earth by thy great power and stretched out arm, and there is nothing too hard for thee.

—JEREMIAH 32:17

PRAYER

Lord God, Thou hast made the heavens and the earth by Thy great power. Thou dost sustain all Thy creation and ordain all Thy purposes. Nothing is too difficult for Thee. Grant my heart, often distracted by many anxieties, a submissive peace that knows by experience Thy limitless power. Grant me the confidence that, if Thou hast accomplished the impossible in the justification of the wicked while remaining just Thyself through the cross of Christ Jesus, Thou canst accomplish all lesser things for Thy people day-to-day. I pray this in our Savior's strong and glorious name. Amen.

BIBLICAL PERSPECTIVE

When the armies of Babylon prepared to destroy Jerusalem, Jeremiah prayed, "Ah Lord GOD! behold, thou hast made the heaven and the earth by thy great power and stretched out arm, and there is nothing too hard for thee" (Jer. 32:17). Jeremiah appealed to God's limitless power.

We call God's infinite power His omnipotence (Latin *omni*, "all," and *potentia*, "power"). James Ussher offered the following summary of divine omnipotence:

- First, He is able to perform whatsoever He will, or that is not contrary to His nature.

- Second, He can do all things without labor, and most easily.

- Third, He can do them either with means, or without means, or contrary to means, as pleases Him.

- Fourth, there is no power which can resist Him.

- Fifth, all power is so in God only, that no creature is able to do anything, but as he does continually receive power from God to do it.[1]

The Lord has infinite power to accomplish all His will and enforce the full rights of His authority. He demonstrated that power in the work of creation, where His mere word of command, "Let there be," brought the world into existence and gave it order (Gen. 1:3, etc.). The majestic heavens express only a "little" of His strength, and "the thunder of his power who can understand?" (Job 26:14).

---

1. Ussher, *A Body of Divinity*, 2nd head (39).

The Lord Jesus is the embodiment of divine power—the "arm of the Lord" hidden in human weakness to save God's people (Isa. 52:10; 53:1–2). Christ is the divine Son of God, "by whom also he made the worlds"—the Son who, throughout history, has been "upholding all things by the word of his power" (Heb. 1:2–3).

At Calvary, we find no miracle such as the Jews sought, but "Christ crucified" is "Christ the power of God" wedded to the exquisite "wisdom of God" (1 Cor. 1:23–24), for by the shame and pain of the cross, Christ conquered sin and Satan (Rom. 6:1–7; Col. 2:14–15). Though God's Son was crucified in human weakness, He rose from the dead in "the power of God" (2 Cor. 13:4), to live by the energy of the Holy Spirit (Rom. 1:4; 8:11), who presently energizes His people to live by faith (Eph. 1:19–22).

The Lord Jesus now exercises universal mediatorial power to give eternal life to God's elect (John 17:2). Each time God regenerates a person unto conversion there is a resurrection of the dead to life (Eph. 2:5), performed by the Spirit. The salvation of a sinner is a new creation (2 Cor. 4:6; 5:17); in fact, it is a greater work than the original creation, for it must overcome the opposition of sin and Satan.[2]

When Christ's disciples questioned who could be saved, the Lord answered, "With men it is impossible, but not with God: for with God all things are possible" (Mark 10:27). Believers are now "kept by the power of God" in their fiery trials (1 Peter 1:5), inwardly strengthened to know Christ's love (Eph. 3:16–19), and empowered to serve in great weakness (2 Cor. 12:9).

---

2. Watson, *A Body of Divinity*, 78.

God's power in Christ will appear openly when people "see the Son of man coming in the clouds with great power and glory" (Mark 13:26). Christ will punish the wicked forever when He reveals "the glory of his power" (2 Thess. 1:9). He will resurrect and glorify His saints with the same divine power by which He Himself rose from the dead (1 Cor. 6:14; Phil. 3:20–21). Just as God showed His power by creating the heaven and the earth, so He will show it again by making a new heaven and a new earth (Isa. 65:17; Rev. 21:1).

The doctrine of God's power has nearly as many applications as there are verses in the Scriptures, for it fills the Bible from beginning to end.

First, God's sovereignty calls us to *trust in His promises*.[3] To the eye of the flesh God's actions seem to be the reverse of His promises. But the eye of faith looks to the Lord omnipotent. It seemed ridiculous that God would give old Abraham and barren Sarah a son, but the Lord gently admonished them, "Is any thing too hard for the Lord?" (Gen. 18:14). Whatever dangers you may face, believe that God is able to sustain you in them or rescue you from them. Such faith is also crucial for your perseverance in sanctification. Watson said, "The strong God can conquer thy strong corruption; though sin be too hard for thee, yet not for him"[4] to forgive by Christ's blood and to conquer by Christ's power.

Second, God's sovereignty calls us to *reverent fear*.[5] Certainly, we may be frightened by men who have the power of

---

3. Ussher, *A Body of Divinity*, 2nd head (42).

4. Watson, *A Body of Divinity*, 81.

5. Watson, *A Body of Divinity*, 79.

armies at their disposal. But much more should we fear the
God who created the stars and planets with His mere word
(Ps. 33:8–9). Few people consider what it would mean for
such a God to be angry with them (90:11). Let us loathe the
thought of provoking Him: "Do we provoke the Lord to
jealousy? are we stronger than he?" (1 Cor. 10:22).[6] Yet the
infinite resources of His power are for those who fear Him,
not against them. We may fear Him with childlike confidence in our heavenly Father.

Third, God's sovereignty calls us to *submission in sorrows*.
When bad news strikes our families, God's grace enables us
to say, "It is the LORD: let him do what seemeth him good"
(1 Sam. 3:18). God has both the right and the power to do
with us as He sees best. Though God's omnipotence grates
harshly on the sufferer's ear when he is in rebellion against
his Maker, this truth enables the saint to repent of his bitter
complaints, put his hand over his mouth, and bow before
the incomprehensible majesty of God (Job 40:1–5; 42:1–6).
Bowing before the Lord who ordains both good and evil in
His righteousness, we experience new hope in God's mercies and faithfulness (Lam. 3:21–29, 37–38).

Fourth, God's sovereignty calls us to *boldness in prayer*.
Paul's prayers for the spiritual growth of the saints are stag-
gering in their high aspirations, but he reminds us that the
Father "is able to do exceeding abundantly above all that we
ask or think" (Eph. 3:20).

---

6. Ezekiel Hopkins, *On Glorifying God in His Attributes*, in *The Works of
the Right Reverend Father in God, Ezekiel Hopkins*, ed. Josiah Pratt (London:
by C. Whittingham, for L. B. Seeley et al., 1809), 3:327.

REFLECTION QUESTIONS

1. Think of the different expressions of human power—political, military, technological, and industrial. How can an exclusive focus on human power be deceptive and dangerous to us?

2. Consider God's power in creation, in redemption by His Son, in the sanctification of sinners by His Spirit, and in bringing about the new creation. How does God's omnipotence help us in every stage of life?

3. Consider Matthew 11:20–21. How is the display of God's power connected with human responsibility to repent of our sins? How has your own repentance been shaped by displays of God's power?

4. Consider 2 Corinthians 12:9. How is the power of Christ made perfect in our "weakness"?

5. Which of the applications of God's omnipotence is the most relevant to your current situation? Why?

DIGGING DEEPER

- Other Scripture passages about God's omnipotence include Exodus 9:16; 1 Chronicles 29:12; Job 42:2; Psalms 33:6, 9; 54:1; 62:11; 106:8; Jeremiah 10:6, 10; 16:21; Daniel 2:20; Matthew 11:5, 20–21, 23; 26:64; Mark 14:36, 62; Luke 1:37; Romans 1:20; 4:21; 1 Corinthians 2:4–5; Ephesians 3:20–21; and Revelation 15:3–4.

- The power of God is intimately related to His other attributes, for they find their vivacity and exercise in His omnipotence. Charnock said, "How vain would be His eternal counsels, if power did not step in to execute them! His mercy would be a feeble pity, if He were destitute of power to relieve; and His justice a slighted scarecrow, without power to punish; His promises an empty sound, without power to accomplish them."[7] God's omnipotence is implied by His other attributes, for He is the infinite Spirit, eternal, self-existent, sufficient, and full of life.

- See also Daniel L. Migliore, *The Power of God and the Gods of Power* (Louisville, Ky.: Westminster John Knox Press, 2008).

---

7. Charnock, *The Existence and Attributes of God*, 2:15.

GOD IS GOOD

23

SCRIPTURE MEDITATION

*And he said, I beseech thee, shew me thy glory.... And the
LORD passed by before him, and proclaimed, The LORD,
The LORD God, merciful and gracious, longsuffering, and
abundant in goodness and truth, keeping mercy for thou-
sands, forgiving iniquity and transgression and sin, and that
will by no means clear the guilty; visiting the iniquity of the
fathers upon the children, and upon the children's children,
unto the third and to the fourth generation.*

—EXODUS 33:18; 34:6–7

PRAYER

Gracious God, Thou art good and Thou doest good.
Thy goodness is truly amazing. Thou hast never *not*
been good to me. Even in times of affliction, Thou
hast never made a mistake in my life. Every trial sent
my way has been marinated in Thy goodness and
intended for both Thy glory and my good. As I meditate upon Thy goodness, wouldst Thou grant me a
fresh understanding and experience of Thy goodness in providence and redemption? Please grant me
an understanding of Thy mercy, grace, patience, and
love that bears the fruit of practical goodness in my

life shown toward others. I pray this in Jesus's name.
Amen.

BIBLICAL PERSPECTIVE

Our meditation upon God's goodness begins with the scene
at Mount Sinai shortly after God had delivered the Israelites
from Egypt with mighty works of judgment and salvation.
Only days after ratifying the covenant, Israel fell into idolatry with the worship of the golden calf, and God's wrath
threatened to destroy the nation (Exodus 32). It appeared
Israel's redemption would end in disaster. However, this
occasion became a wondrous display of God's mercy
and grace (Exodus 33–34). When Moses interceded for
idolatrous Israel, he prayed, "Shew my thy glory," and in
response, God expressed His "goodness" (Ex. 33:18–19) in a
list of attributes that begins with mercy, grace, patience, and
goodness (Ex. 34:6). Let us consider the manifold display of
God's *goodness* mentioned in these attributes.

God's mercy in the Old Testament expresses the compassion of a mother (or father) for a child (cf. Isa. 49:15). That
God is merciful means that He is not insensitive to us in our
weaknesses and troubles, but responds to our miseries with
tender pity (Ps. 116:3–5; Isa. 49:10). Likewise, in the New
Testament, God's mercy is His active compassion toward us
in our misery (Matt. 15:22; Luke 16:24).

Whereas mercy emphasizes the kindness shown to
someone in misery, *grace* stresses free generosity to someone to whom the giver owes nothing—such as the poor.[1]

---

1. Turretin, *Institutes*, 3.20.7, 10 (1:242–43); and Feinberg, *No One
Like Him*, 359.

In the context of Exodus 33–34, God's grace is His favor to those whom He knows, forgives, and grants His special presence (Ex. 33:12–13, 16–17; 34:9). In Paul's letters, God's grace is His loving purpose and active power to save sinners through Christ.[2] Grace establishes God's sovereign freedom to save whom He chooses and it opposes salvation by the merit of man's works (Rom. 4:4–5; 11:5–6; Gal. 2:15–21; Titus 3:3–7).

God's *patience* is described in Exodus 34:6 as His being "longsuffering." God is "longsuffering" because He is slow to anger. He desires to seek peace and forgive rather than retaliate quickly (Num. 14:18; Neh. 9:17). He reserves His wrath until the right time to execute justice (Nah. 1:2–3). God patiently waits while sinners grow more wicked, despise His warnings, abuse His goodness, insult His holy name, and all the while accuse Him of wrongdoing. Paul warns the impenitent that if they continue to despise God's "riches of his goodness and forbearance and longsuffering," they store up greater measures of wrath for themselves on judgment day (Rom. 2:4–5).

God's goodness is displayed in His *love*. When the Lord says He is "abundant in goodness" (Ex. 34:6), the word rendered as "goodness" is more often translated as "loving-kindness" (KJV) or "steadfast love" (ESV). By sending His Son to die for lawless, wicked men, God demonstrated both His love (Rom. 5:6–10) and His righteousness (Rom. 3:25–26), for Christ bore the curse of the law to satisfy divine justice (Gal. 3:10, 13). God holds a special love for believers,

---

2. Herman Ridderbos, *Paul: An Outline of His Theology*, trans. John Richard de Witt (Grand Rapids: Eerdmans, 1975), 173.

even as He has loved His Son (John 17:23). Thus, in Christ, God's love is steadfast, covenantal, and eternal.

God's goodness is a wide and fertile field in which human piety and justice grow. It is the vital heartbeat of God's image. Knowing God's goodness and making it known is the central purpose for which we exist. Therefore, it calls for you to respond.

First, *have absolute confidence that God is good*. Trust Him and believe that those who trust in such a good God are blessed by Him (Ps. 34:8). Trust in Christ as the supreme example of God's love and the only Mediator by whom you will be saved by His love (1 John 4:9–10).

Second, *ground your confidence in God's goodness upon Christ*. Look to the cross for irrefutable proof that God loves you, and when God's providence hurts you deeply, see in Christ's hands and His side the marks of His love. In the shadow of the cross, patiently bear your sorrows with confidence that He will give you all good things and work all things for your good (Rom. 8:28, 31–32).[3]

Third, *love God for His goodness* (Luke 7:47; 1 John 4:19). God's goodness displays His loveliness: "For how great is his goodness, and how great is his beauty!" (Zech. 9:17).[4] Witsius said that the love of God "kindles surprising flames of reciprocal love."[5]

Fourth, *receive His good gifts with gratitude and holiness* (1 Tim. 4:3–5). If you do not glorify Him for His gifts,

---

3. Charnock, *The Existence and Attributes of God*, 2:350.

4. Charnock, *The Existence and Attributes of God*, 2:330.

5. Herman Witsius, *Sacred Dissertations on the Apostles' Creed*, trans. Donald Fraser (1823; repr., Grand Rapids: Reformation Heritage Books, 2010), 1:117.

He may take them back (Hos. 2:8–9). Fear to abuse God's goodness with ingratitude, complaining, and contempt for God the giver, lest God give you over to inner darkness and depravity (Rom. 1:21), and damn you on the last day (Rom. 2:4–5).[6]

Fifth, *desire God as your supreme good*. Meditate prayerfully on the love of God until, as à Brakel said, your soul is increasingly "irradiated by the love of God and ignited with reciprocal love," so that your heart "no longer covets the love of others and is readily weaned from all that appears to be desirable upon earth."[7]

Sixth, *love others fervently and sacrificially in the church of Christ* (Eph. 4:32; 1 Peter 1:22). The gospel both reveals God's love and enjoins us to love each other as God loved us (1 John 4:10–11). Do not rest upon inward wishes of love; examine yourself for practical fruits of love. How has love cost you time, money, and energy? John says, "Let us not love in word, neither in tongue; but in deed and in truth" (1 John 3:18).

Seventh, *worship God for His goodness and love*. This was the response of Moses when the Lord proclaimed His goodness and the greatness of His love: "And Moses made haste, and bowed his head toward the earth, and worshipped" (Ex. 34:8).[8] Let us "be thankful unto him and bless his name, For the LORD is good; his mercy is everlasting; and his truth endureth to all generations" (Ps. 100:4–5). How can those of us whom He bought with His blood do any less?

---

6. Charnock, *The Existence and Attributes of God*, 2:313–15.

7. Wilhelmus à Brakel, *The Christian's Reasonable Service*, trans. Bartel Elshout, ed. Joel R. Beeke (Grand Rapids: Reformation Heritage Books, 1992–1995), 1:134–35.

8. Nichols, *Lectures in Systematic Theology*, 1:466.

REFLECTION QUESTIONS

1. What are the different aspects of God's goodness, according to Exodus 34:6, and how do each of these work in your life?

2. What are some of the reasons that you can have absolute confidence in God's goodness?

3. What are some concrete ways in your life that God's goodness—His loveliness—has caused you to love Him more?

4. According to Romans 1:18–32, what are some of the consequences of failing to give thanks to God for His goodness and His generous gifts?

5. Consider how you can imitate God's goodness in all things—showing kindness even to the plants and animals that God created,[9] and loving even your enemies (Matt. 5:44–45). Shall God's heart be large and open to you, but your heart be narrow and closed to others?[10]

---

9. Deut. 5:14; 20:19; 22:6–7; 25:4; Prov. 12:10.

10. Charnock, *The Existence and Attributes of God*, 2:353.

DIGGING DEEPER

- Here are some other Scripture passages about God's goodness (Pss. 31:19; 34:8; 119:68; James 1:17); mercy (Ps. 103:13–14; Lam. 3:22–23; Matt. 17:15; Luke 17:13; Phil. 2:27); grace (Eph. 1:4–6; 2:8–9; 2 Tim. 1:9); patience (Neh. 9:30; Ps. 86:15; Isa. 48:9; Joel 2:13); and love (Ezra 3:11; Pss. 100:5; 106:1; 107:1; 118:1–4, 29; 136:1–26; Jer. 31:3, 31; 33:11; Rom. 8:29; Eph. 1:6).

- All of God's *moral* attributes may be summarized by "goodness." Just as the Creator transcends the creature in His aseity, infinity, and immutability (His *greatness*), God is the *supreme good*. In His own being He is good of Himself, infinitely and unchangeably good.[11] To have God is to have the supreme good, even if every other good is taken away (Pss. 4:6–7; 73:25–28; Hab. 3:17–19).[12] God's goodness can fill your soul with sweet joy when you have an assurance that this God is *your* God. Herman Witsius said that the believer finds in God "an inexhaustible fountain of all desirable good; not only what equals, but also what infinitely transcends his conceptions and desires" (cf. Ps. 36:7–9).[13]

---

11. Augustine, *Concerning the Nature of Good, against the Manichaens*, chap. 1, in *A Select Library of Nicene and Post-Nicene Fathers of the Christian Church*, ed. Philip Schaff (New York: Christian Literature, 1888), 4:351; and Charnock, *The Existence and Attributes of God*, 2:210–11. See Augustine, *On the Trinity*, 3:117–18.

12. Bavinck, *Reformed Dogmatics*, 2:212.

13. Herman Witsius, *Sacred Dissertations on the Apostles' Creed*, trans. Donald Fraser (1823; repr., Grand Rapids: Reformation Heritage Books, 2010), 1:111.

- God's faithful love is the source of our hope of forgiveness (Neh. 9:17). God's love enables us to approach Him and worship in His presence with reverent fear (Ps. 5:7). God's love endures "forever" (1 Chron. 16:34, 41; 2 Chron. 5:13; 7:3, 6; 20:21). In His love God pursues elect sinners as a husband pursues an unfaithful wife to bring her back to Himself (Hos. 3:1; cf. Isa. 54:1–10). He chooses to "love them freely" so that their backsliding is healed, His anger is propitiated, and His divine vitality makes them fruitful (Hos. 14:4–8). Praise God for His relentless, pursuing love of sinners!

- See also Megan Hill, *Contentment: Seeing God's Goodness* (Phillipsburg, N.J.: P&R, 2018); Rebecca Stark, *The Good Portion—God: The Doctrine of God for Every Woman* (Fern, Ross-shire, Scotland: Christian Focus, 2018).

24

GOD IS LOVE

SCRIPTURE MEDITATION

And we have known and believed the love that God hath to us. God is love; and he that dwelleth in love dwelleth in God, and God in him.

—1 JOHN 4:16

PRAYER

Glorious, triune God, as I begin this meditation on Thy love, gently remind me of Thy great love for me. Remind me that Thou hast so loved the world, that Thou gavest Thy only Son, Jesus Christ. Give me a fresh perspective on Thy love and help me to be amazed at how faithful it is, how true it is, and how enduring it is. Help me to realize that I can never fathom the breadth and depth of the ocean of Thy love, even as I swim in its fullness. I pray this in the strong name of Jesus, my loving Lord. Amen.

BIBLICAL PERSPECTIVE

Love isn't just an attribute of God; it's His very nature. From all eternity the Father, Son, and Holy Spirit are held in a perfect unity of love. In fact, this is one of the reasons

Jesus says in His prayer before His arrest that the Father loved Him "before the foundation of the world" (John 17:24). Paul writes that we, as God's elect, are blessed in Christ Jesus, "the beloved" (Eph. 1:6).

We may appropriately call God "the God of love." As you meditate on the God of love, rest in His Word: "And the Lord direct your hearts into the love of God, and into the patient waiting for Christ" (2 Thess. 3:5). Stop and pray that this may be true of your own heart this day.

There are several amazing truths surrounding our passage for today in the fourth chapter of 1 John. First, John teaches us that love is from God (1 John 4:7). Any streams of love we exhibit come from the deep and wide ocean of divine love.

Second, John points to the greatest expression of love: "In this was manifested the love of God toward us, because that God sent his only begotten Son into the world, that we might live through him" (v. 9). This, of course, echoes Romans 5:8, where Paul explains, "But God commendeth his love toward us, in that, while we were yet sinners, Christ died for us." The incarnation—God taking on flesh in the person of Jesus Christ resulting in the life, death, and work of Christ—is the greatest witness and display of divine love.

A third contextual truth surrounding our passage is that God's love is "perfected in us" (1 John 4:12). The word in Greek for "perfected" here is the same word used by Jesus on the cross when He proclaimed, "It is finished" (John 19:30). Not only was our debt *paid in full*, but God's love for us was also *paid in full*. There can be nothing added to or taken away from God's love for us. In other words, there is no more love to be "used up." His love is also unconditional; it cannot waver or fail. Because God's character is unchanging and because His love is based on His unchanging character, *His love is unchanging.*

Fourth, John teaches, "There is no fear in love; but perfect love casteth out fear" (1 John 4:18). Perfect love isn't referring to *our* love, but to *God's* love. He is the only One with perfect love and He casts out our fear of others, of death, and of sin. If you know deep down that you are unconditionally loved by the King of the universe, what is there to fear? Death has been swallowed up in victory (1 Cor. 15:54)!

Fifth, "we love him, because he first loved us" (1 John 4:19). The only way men, women, boys, and girls can ever love God is if God first gives them new hearts to love Him (Ezek. 36:26). Our love is our response to His gracious love in the first place.

The final contextual truth surrounding our text for today is that "we ought also to love one another" (1 John 4:11). Our love should reflect the love of God. When asked about the greatest commandment, Jesus responded, "Thou shalt love the Lord thy God with all thy heart, and with all thy soul, and with all thy mind" (Matt. 22:37). But He followed this answer with the *second* greatest commandment, "Thou shalt love thy neighbour as thyself" (v. 39). If we have been so loved by God, saved through the work of Christ, and sealed by the Holy Spirit (Eph. 1:13), then we should abound in our love for one another (1 Thess. 3:12).

REFLECTION QUESTIONS

1. As you reflect on our passage in 1 John 4:16, do you see any difference between believing *in* the love of God and simply believing the love of God?

2. How would you define *love*? Would your definition match the biblical perspective given in this chapter?

3. John teaches that "God is love." Can love be love if it is not expressed or given to another?

4. By the Spirit's grace, take a few minutes to meditate on and abide in God's love. Rest in the knowledge that He loves *you* unconditionally, even right after you sin against Him. Let your affections be stirred by God's amazing love for you.

5. What are some practical ways that you can "abide in God's love" on a regular basis?

6. How can the truth that "God is love" give you strength to love one another?

DIGGING DEEPER

- Some other Scripture passages on the love of God include Exodus 34:6; 2 Chronicles 5:13; Psalm 100:5; Jeremiah 31:3; John 3:16–17; 15:13; Romans 5:8; 8:35–39; 1 Corinthians 13; 2 Corinthians 5:14; Galatians 5:22; Ephesians 2:4; 5:2–25; Philippians 1:9; Colossians 3:14; 2 Thessalonians 2:16; 1 John 4; and Revelation 1:5.

- Discipline and love actually go together for the believer. Consider Hebrews 12:6, "For whom the Lord loveth he chasteneth." Believer, do not think your suffering is from wrath, but from love; it is not judicially pronounced against you by God, but is medicinally designed for you by Him.

- Paul explains that we are to grow in our love *with knowledge*. "And this I pray, that your love may abound yet more and more in knowledge and in all judgment" (Phil. 1:9). Jonathan Edwards once noted that our worship should have heat in the heart and light in the mind, but no more heat than justified by the light. What do you think he is communicating by saying that?

- See also John Piper, *Think: The Life of the Mind and the Love of God* (Wheaton, Ill.: Crossway, 2010); David Powlison, *God's Love: Better Than Unconditional* (Phillipsburg, N.J.: P&R, 2001); D. A. Carson, *The Difficult Doctrine of the Love of God* (Wheaton, Ill.: Crossway, 2000).

25

GOD IS GRACIOUS

SCRIPTURE MEDITATION

I will make all my goodness pass before thee, and I will proclaim the name of the LORD before thee; and will be gracious to whom I will be gracious, and will shew mercy on whom I will shew mercy.

—EXODUS 33:19

PRAYER

Gracious, heavenly Father, I do not deserve life or salvation. I don't deserve *anything* but death and hell forever. But Thou art gracious and merciful. It is by Thy grace alone that I am saved and can enjoy fellowship with Thee and with other believers in Christ. In fact, grace does everything for me and gives everything needed to me. May Thy grace amaze me now as I peer into this attribute of Thy perfect character. Please let Thy Spirit expand the elasticity of my soul to take in more and more of Thee and to rest in Thy grace this day, for the sake of Thy Son in whose name I pray. Amen.

BIBLICAL PERSPECTIVE

Many people today have a sense of entitlement. They might say things like, "I am entitled to this car or that house." "I deserve a higher-paying job or perfect grades in my classes." If you listen much to modern media, you know that advertisements are geared toward making you believe that you are entitled to whatever product they are trying to sell. They would have us believe that it is right—even "just"—for us to simply have whatever we want, as if we *deserve* it.

But the biblical message gives an entirely different picture. When it speaks of what we deserve, the payment is vastly different. Consider the nature of our sinful hearts:

> God saw that the wickedness of man was great in the earth, and that every imagination of the thoughts of his heart was only evil continually. (Gen. 6:5)

> There is none that doeth good, no, not one. (Ps. 14:3)

> The heart is deceitful above all things. (Jer. 17:9)

> And you...were dead in trespasses and sins. (Eph. 2:1)

> For all have sinned, and come short of the glory of God. (Rom. 3:23)

> For the wages of sin is death. (Rom. 6:23)

It is clear from Scripture that all are sinful, lost, and without hope except in the sovereign grace of God. All deserve His divine wrath and judgment. In other words, it would be *fair* if everyone went to hell. But God is gracious and gives us what we don't deserve.

There is a subtle difference between grace and mercy. To be sure, God is both gracious and merciful. But the biblical view of saving grace is narrow and reserved only for His chosen people, the elect. A. W. Pink explains, "Grace is a perfection of the divine character which is exercised only toward the elect." He goes on to say, "Neither in the Old Testament nor in the New is the grace of God ever mentioned in connection with mankind generally."[1] Notwithstanding, the rain falls on the just and the unjust alike (Matt. 5:45). God showers earthly blessing on believers and unbelievers alike, which is a truth often referred to as God's *common grace.*

God's "tender mercies" are, on the other hand, "over all his works" (Ps. 145:9). Mercy is God not giving you what you deserve, or at least giving you a temporary relief from what you deserve. It is only by His mercy that all of mankind isn't consumed immediately by divine wrath and justice. Believers, then, receive *both* grace and mercy.

The grace of God is His sovereign unmerited favor upon His sheep, the church, which is the bride of Christ. Because grace is an attribute of God's character, it is eternal—even before it was actually extended to His people. Paul explains that God saved us, "not according to our works, but according to his own purpose and grace, which was given us in Christ Jesus before the world began" (2 Tim. 1:9).

God's grace is also sovereign, given only to those whom He chooses. As God says in our passage for today, "[I] will be gracious to whom I will be gracious, and will shew mercy on whom I will shew mercy" (Ex. 33:19). God is completely sovereign to bestow divine favor on whomever He chooses.

---

1. Pink, *The Attributes of God*, 66.

God's grace is also a gift, which means that it is received freely apart from any payment of our own. Paul writes, "For by grace are ye saved through faith; and that not of yourselves: it is the gift of God" (Eph. 2:8). Though the gift of grace costs you nothing, it cost Jesus His life. Jesus took your wages of sin upon Himself so that you would receive the wages of righteousness and the gift of eternal life.

One of the purposes of God's law[2] is to show how sinful we truly are, which only highlights the wonder of grace all the more: "Moreover the law entered, that the offence might abound. But where sin abounded, grace did much more abound" (Rom. 5:20).

Finally, we are to "grow in grace, and in the knowledge of our Lord and Saviour Jesus Christ" (2 Peter 3:18). Although we are counted completely forgiven and righteous through faith in Jesus, God continues to transform us daily until we reach the "fulness of Christ" (Eph. 4:13). It is by grace alone that we are saved. It is by grace alone that we find joy and hope in the gospel of Christ. It is by grace alone that "we live, and move, and have our being" (Acts 17:28). It is by grace alone that God pardons our sin and accepts us as righteous in His sight. And it is by grace alone that He will usher us one day into glory.

---

2. Historically, theologians have distinguished three "uses" of the law of God. First, the law restrains evil and sin in society. Without laws society could not function, but would break out into anarchy. Second, the law convicts us of sin and shows us the depths of our sin—this is the evangelical or didactic use of the law that uncovers our need for Christ. Third, the law reveals to us what pleases God, so that God's people love it and use it as a rule of life by which they show their gratitude to God through humble and sincere obedience.

REFLECTION QUESTIONS

1. Are there things that you believe you "deserve" or are entitled to? Think honestly about this question.

2. In our Scripture passage for today, why do you think God's name, "The LORD," is important as we consider God's grace? What about that title reveals more of the nature of God's grace?

3. Right now, can you think of how God is showing you *mercy* specifically? What is He withholding that you really deserve?

4. Take a few minutes to consider the depths of your sin. Do you see it for what it is, as cosmic treason against your Creator and Sustainer? Consider God's grace in saving you from your sin—placing that sin upon His only Son, who died in your place. What should your response be to such amazing grace?

5. Do you ever think that you deserve God's blessing and favor more than another person? Are there people who you think simply don't deserve any grace at all? Do you think that you deserve that grace?

6. How can you practically extend grace to people at work or school, or to family members—especially when they have hurt you?

7. How does the gospel of grace give you the *right motivation* to serve God and others?

DIGGING DEEPER

- Some other Scripture passages on the God of grace include Psalms 86:15; 103:8; 116:5; Amos 5:15; John 1:14; Acts 15:11; Romans 3:24; 5:20; 1 Corinthians 15:10; 2 Corinthians 8:9; 12:9; Ephesians 1:6; 2:8; Titus 2:11; 1 Peter 1:13; 5:10; and 2 Peter 3:18.

- If we think that grace is "deserved" it is no longer grace we are talking about. Grace is never deserved, but given freely by God who is sovereign. We not only have not merited grace; we are not even neutral to grace, for we have "de-merited" it. That is to say, we have merited, by nature, nothing but death and hell.

- See also Sinclair Ferguson, *By Grace Alone: How the Grace of God Amazes Me* (Lake Mary, Fla.: Reformation Trust Publishing, 2010); Jerry Bridges, *The Discipline of Grace: God's Role and Our Role in the Pursuit of Holiness* (Colorado Springs, Colo.: NavPress, 2006); Charles Spurgeon, *Grace: God's Unmerited Favor* (New Kensington, Pa.: Whitaker House, 1996).

26

GOD IS TRUTH

SCRIPTURE MEDITATION

This then is the message which we have heard of him, and declare unto you, that God is light, and in him is no darkness at all.... If we confess our sins, he is faithful and just to forgive us our sins, and to cleanse us from all unrighteousness.
—1 JOHN 1:5, 9

PRAYER

God of truth, giver of truth, and lover of truth: Thy truth and faithfulness are the solid bedrock of all Thy creation, providence, and promises. Thy word and works are true. Help me to fight the good fight of confronting the lies from this world and even from my own sinful nature. Make Thy truth speak in my life louder than falsehood. Grant me grace to buy the truth and refuse to sell it. Assist me each day to love and live the truth as flowing out of Thy Son, who is the way, the truth, and the life. Help me always to run to Thy reliable, illuminating, and steadfast promises, and to Thy Son, the incarnation of Thy promise and faithfulness. I pray this in the name of Jesus, who is ever faithful and true. Amen.

BIBLICAL PERSPECTIVE

We now turn to consider God's moral excellence from the perspectives of His truth and righteousness. The Song of Moses provides us with a rich summary of these facets of God's moral excellence: "He is the Rock, his work is perfect: for all his ways are judgment: a God of truth and without iniquity, just and right is he" (Deut. 32:4). God is the unchangeable, solid Rock, "the standard, the criterion of all things," as Herman Hoeksema said.[1] John writes, "God is light, and in him is no darkness at all" (1 John 1:5). In that context, John connects light with truth (vv. 6, 8). John also says, "He is faithful" (v. 9). Let us turn to meditate upon God's truth and faithfulness.

That God is true means that He is the real, solid, unchanging "Rock"; He is the "God of truth" (Deut. 32:4). In the context of Deuteronomy 32, "God of truth" not only counts Him as faithful but contrasts Him with the false gods of the nations: "For their rock is not as our Rock.... Where are their gods, their rock in whom they trusted?" (vv. 31, 37). Likewise, the New Testament's testimony that God is the "true" God is a reference to His unique reality as the living and life-giving God in contrast to false gods and impotent idols (1 John 5:20–21).

God is "truth" in three senses: First, God is truth in the world's *metaphysical sense of reality*: He is the true God as opposed to all false and unreal deities. Second, God is truth in the *logical sense of accuracy*: He is the living and eternal wisdom who knows all things as they are, and His words

---

1. Herman Hoeksema, *Reformed Dogmatics*, 2nd ed. (Grandville, Mich.: Reformed Free Publishing Association, 2004), 1:175.

are without error. Third, God is truth in the *ethical sense of fidelity*: He lives, speaks, and acts with unfailing faithfulness, consistency, and moral integrity.[2]

The promise of eternal life in the gospel of Christ is founded upon the truth of God. God accomplishes this great salvation by the King promised in the Davidic covenant. This promise rests upon the solid bedrock of God's faithfulness and is executed by the strong arm of His power (2 Sam. 7:12–16, 28; Isa. 55:3). We know that God's covenantal promises are certain, for they are confirmed by His faithfulness in maintaining the succession of day, night, and the seasons—as He promised in His covenant with Noah (Gen. 8:21–22; 9:8–11).

In fulfillment of God's promises, Christ came as the incarnation of God's faithfulness: "But as God is true, our word toward you was not yea and nay…. For all the promises of God in him are yea, and in him Amen, unto the glory of God by us" (2 Cor. 1:18–20).

Jesus says "I am…the truth" (John 14:6). Christ, then, is the totally accurate and reliable revelation of God, the glorious Word of the Father (John 1:1, 14). Christ is "the true Light" that gives life to men (v. 9); "the true bread from heaven," of which manna was only a shadow (6:32); and "the true vine" (15:1), in union with whom you can bear spiritual fruit. The Father and the Son send the Spirit of truth, so called because He bears witness to Christ's glory in the writings of the apostles in contrast to the errors of this world (John 16:13). The "anointing" of the Spirit

---

2. Bavinck, *Reformed Dogmatics*, 2:209.

enables people to know God, for it "is truth, and is no lie" (1 John 2:27).

The truthfulness of God should have a manifold effect in our lives.

First, you can *be certain that the words of God are reliable*, for they are "true and faithful" (Rev. 21:5), "what the Spirit saith" (Rev. 2:7), and the very "word of truth" (Eph. 1:13).

Second, *you can trust God and let your soul take its rest in Him*, for the One who *created* you and *called* you is faithful (1 Peter 4:19; 1 Cor. 1:9). God is faithful to help you bear temptation, and if you do fall, He is faithful and just to forgive you if you confess your sins (1 Cor. 10:13; 1 John 1:9). Does your faith answer to God's faithfulness? There is no one worthier of your trust.

Third, God's faithfulness calls you *to repent of your unbelief*. Greg Nichols warns, "Unbelief and skepticism call God a liar. When sinners reject his testimony, they insult his truthfulness."[3] When dark circumstances, doubts, and hard feelings militate against your confidence in God, does your soul rest upon the bare Word of God? Or are you shaken and tossed about like a leaf in the wind? Meditate upon God's attribute of truth. Consider how He has proven Himself faithful again and again, especially in the incarnation and work of Jesus Christ. Trust Christ.

Fourth, God's truth calls us to *pray for more grace and peace*. Isaiah 26:3 says, "Thou wilt keep him in perfect peace, whose mind is stayed on thee: because he trusteth in thee." Fight for that peace by fixing your mind on the faithful God, the Rock of His people.

---

3. Nichols, *Lectures in Systematic Theology*, 1:539.

REFLECTION QUESTIONS

1. How did God demonstrate His truth by the incarnation and work of Jesus Christ?

2. We saw that God is truth in three senses: *metaphysical* truth, *logical* truth, and *ethical* truth. Explain the critical need we have for each of these as we face many "versions" of truth today.

3. In our postmodern context, truth is seen as relative, changeable according to personal preference, constructed and subjective, rather than revealed and objective. What Scripture specifically helps you respond to a view of truth as relative?

4. Think about the connection between God's truth and our trust. How can a better understanding of God's truth help you trust Him more?

5. Which of the applications in this meditation on the truth of God is most applicable to your current situation? How?

DIGGING DEEPER

- Other Scripture passages about God's truth include Psalms 31:5; 86:15; Isaiah 65:16; Jeremiah 10:10; John 15:26; 16:13; 17:3; 1 Thessalonians 1:9; and 1 John 4:6.

- Truth as a personal attribute is an ethical quality that overlaps with love and righteousness. "Truth" is often paired with God's faithful love (Hebrew, *khesed*). "Withhold not thou thy tender mercies from me, O LORD: let thy lovingkindness and thy truth continually preserve me" (Ps. 40:11; cf. Pss. 25:10; 57:3, 10; 85:10; 89:14; 108:4; 115:1; 117:2; 138:2; Mic. 7:20).

- The Hebrew adverb rendered as "verily" (*'amen*) means "I agree wholeheartedly," "let it be so," or "may it come true."[4] In the New Testament, the term transliterated into Greek (*amēn*) often appears on the lips of Jesus Christ to indicate the truthfulness of His sayings (Matt. 5:18; John 1:51). The Lord is named, literally, "the God of truth" (Isa. 65:16), and Christ called Himself "the Amen, the faithful and true witness" (Rev. 3:14). William Perkins commented that Christ's word is "authentic, sufficient of itself, and needs no other confirmation," for "he speaks the truth, according as everything is in itself, without error, deceit, or falsehood, for that which he receives [is] from his Father, which is the rule of all truth."[5]

- See also Kelly Minter, *Finding God Faithful* (Nashville, Tenn.: Broadman & Holman, 2019).

---

4. Deut. 27:15–26; 1 Kings 1:36; 1 Chron. 16:36; Neh. 5:13; Pss. 41:13; 72:19; 89:52; 106:48. Jer. 11:5; 28:6.

5. William Perkins, *A Godly and Learned Exposition or Commentary upon the Three First Chapters of the Revelation*, in *The Works of William Perkins*, ed. Stephen Yuille (Grand Rapids: Reformation Heritage Books, 2017), 4:334, 595.

27

GOD IS FAITHFUL

SCRIPTURE MEDITATION

And the very God of peace sanctify you wholly; and I pray God your whole spirit and soul and body be preserved blameless unto the coming of our Lord Jesus Christ. Faithful is he that calleth you, who also will do it.

—1 THESSALONIANS 5:23–24

PRAYER

Faithful Father, I praise Thee that Thou art perfectly committed to me, even when I am not committed to Thee. I thank Thee for Thy steadfast love and faithfulness to Thy children and that Thou wilt never let us go. Thou wilt never leave us nor forsake us. As I look now to this attribute of Thy faithfulness and meditate upon it, wouldst Thou expose sins that I am harboring and bring me to a place of delight in Thy grace? Apply Thy holy Word to my life this day, for Christ's sake. Amen.

BIBLICAL PERSPECTIVE

Since the mid-1900s, America has witnessed a rapid breakdown of the family. Almost half of Americans polled today don't believe that marriage is even necessary. Many think that marriage is simply about "feeling" love, rather than commitment in a bound relationship for the glory of God. We are taught to be committed to something only so long as we are happy. It's all about our happiness and good feelings, rather than to reflect the covenant-keeping relationship between Christ and His bride (Eph. 5:25–32).

Church life is no different. As soon as we don't like the positioning of the tables, the smell of the flowers, the sound of the piano, or the length of the sermon, we begin looking around for a church that will suit our tastes. In other words, commitment is thrown to the back seat and personal preference drives the course of our relationships. The irony, of course, is that commitment shines brightest in times of suffering, hardship, and difficulty. That's why wedding vows include being rich *and* poor, health *and* sickness, for better *or* for worse. It's in the hard times that commitment is seen most clearly.

God understands commitment and faithfulness fully because it is part of His character. Throughout the Old Testament, Israel played the part of the prostitute—turning after "lovers" of this world rather than resting in the true Lover of her soul (Ezekiel 16; Hosea 2). But God remained faithful to them. He was loyal, steadfast, committed, and bound to them—despite Israel's great *un*faithfulness to Him.

One of the clearest expressions of this is seen in the Hebrew word, *chesed*, which is translated into English as "mercy," "loyal love," "steadfast love," "unfailing love," "committed love," or "covenant love." Consider these passages from the Psalter:

> All the paths of the LORD are mercy and truth unto such as keep his covenant and his testimonies. (Ps. 25:10)

> For thou, Lord, art good, and ready to forgive; and plenteous in mercy unto all them that call upon thee. (Ps. 86:5)

> Justice and judgment are the habitation of thy throne: mercy and truth shall go before thy face. (Ps. 89:14)

> O satisfy us early with thy mercy; that we may rejoice and be glad all our days. (Ps. 90:14)

> For the LORD is good; his mercy is everlasting; and his truth endureth to all generations. (Ps. 100:5)

> For his merciful kindness is great toward us: and the truth of the LORD endureth for ever. (Ps. 117:2)

Notice the close relationship between God's "mercy" or "steadfast love" (*chesed*) and God's "faithfulness." God's love doesn't fail. It doesn't ebb and flow with the tide of emotions. God's covenant promise is that He will remain our God and we will remain His people (Ex. 6:7; Jer. 30:22).

One of the greatest rewards of commitment and faithfulness is *intimacy*. Having an intimate relationship with somebody means knowing them—faults and all—and loving them anyway. It's the wonderful effect of a harmonious blend of knowledge and love. God seeks intimate fellowship with His people. He knows us completely and loves us *anyway* because we are "in Christ." The amazing thing about the gospel is that God gets glory when we find our satisfaction and joy in Him. We experience intimacy with Him when we know Him and love Him because of the fact that He has first known and loved us (1 John 4:19).

Your love for God follows your knowledge of God. Therefore, let the knowledge of God's faithfulness draw your affections toward Him and you will find deep and satisfying intimacy with the Lover of your soul!

The more and more you rest in the faithfulness of God, the more faithfulness will be evidenced as a fruit of the Spirit in your own life (Gal. 5:22). The more you trust in God's faithfulness to forgive sin (1 John 1:9), the more you will find strength to fight sin. The more you look unto God's faithfulness *in* your suffering, the more you will find peace, comfort, and joy. Consider Jeremiah's praise in the midst of suffering: "It is of the LORD's mercies that we are not consumed, because his compassions fail not. They are new every morning: great is thy faithfulness" (Lam. 3:22–23). God's faithfulness gives believers the right motivation and resource to pursue a life of faithfulness to Him.

REFLECTION QUESTIONS

1. Have you ever battled the same sin over and over? You might have even made a promise to God that you would "never do that again!" How might reflecting on God's faithfulness to you give you spiritual strength to resist this sin in the future?

2. In 1 Thessalonians 5:23, God promises to sanctify you completely. That means that, until you reach heaven, you will always need grace. The promise is sure, but

the journey is ahead. Can you see real, tangible signs of growth in your own Christian journey?

3. Our text says, "Faithful is he that calleth you." God never efficaciously calls anyone without also giving them the resources to finish the race. What are some resources that God has given us to grow in our knowledge of and love for God?

4. How can the truth of God's faithful, steadfast love comfort your soul?

5. Do you have any truly intimate friendships with people who know the good, the bad, and the ugly about you and love you *anyway*? What might hinder you from building such a relationship?

6. Jesus Christ was perfectly faithful in keeping all of God's commandments and laws—*on your behalf,* dear believer. The credit and merit of His perfect obedience is credited to you by simply believing in Him alone as your Savior and Lord. How might this truth free you from pretending to be a "good" Christian all of the time?

DIGGING DEEPER

- Some other Scripture passages on God's faithfulness include Numbers 23:19; Deuteronomy 7:9; Psalms 36:5; 86:15; 100:5; 117:2; 145:13; Isaiah 11:5; 49:7; Lamentations 3:22–23; 1 Corinthians 1:9; 10:13; 2 Thessalonians 3:3; 2 Timothy 2:19; Hebrews 10:23; 1 Peter 4:19; 1 John 1:9; and Revelation 19:11.

- A lack of personal faithfulness is ultimately a lack of faith. If you had great faith in the greatness of the gospel, you would have greater faithfulness toward God. If you find that your faithfulness is more unfaithful than you would like, avail yourself of the means of God's transformative grace: God's Word, the reading of biblically sound literature, prayer, the sacraments, spiritual fellowship, service, and grace-driven community.

- See also E. Calvin Beisner, *Psalms of Promise: Celebrating the Majesty and Faithfulness of God* (Phillipsburg, N.J.: P&R, 1994).

28

GOD IS JUST

SCRIPTURE MEDITATION

Because I will publish the name of the LORD: ascribe ye greatness unto our God. He is the Rock, his work is perfect: for all his ways are judgment: a God of truth and without iniquity, just and right is he.

—DEUTERONOMY 32:3–4

PRAYER

Heavenly Father, as I quiet my mind and heart now to consider and ponder Thy justice, wouldst Thou remind me of the payment for my sin in the death of Christ—that He bore Thy wrath to satisfy Thy justice in punishing sin—yes, *my* sin in particular? I am grateful that Thou art a just God, calling me to do justice, to love kindness, and to walk humbly with Thee. Please teach me more of Thy just character so that I would understand more about Thy perfect grace, displayed in the gospel of Thy Son, Jesus. Hear me, with the pardoning of all my sins, through Christ's atoning blood. Amen.

BIBLICAL PERSPECTIVE

That God is *just* can be understood in two related ways. First, justice is a virtue of God in that He is an equitable Lord. The moral bar of this attribute is His righteousness. God is just in that He has perfect integrity of moral character and righteous virtue. Sin, therefore, cannot be tolerated or go unpunished under His sovereign rule. Consider Romans 1:32: "Who knowing the judgment of God, that they which commit such things are worthy of death, not only do the same, but have pleasure in them that do them."

The second way that we understand God's justice is in how He *expresses* His just character—as either reward or punishment. As the psalmist declares, "The king's strength also loveth judgment; thou dost establish equity, thou executest judgment and righteousness in Jacob" (Ps. 99:4). Or consider Paul's teaching in Romans 2:6, that God "will render to every man according to his deeds."

In view of God who rewards the obedient, the reward is not based on strict merit, but according to His promises of His grace and agreement. That is why Isaiah calls our righteousness "filthy rags" (Isa. 64:6). God is a Rewarder because He is the God who is faithful to His own promises and clothes us with *His* righteousness by faith (cf. Gen. 15:6; Isa. 61:10; Phil. 3:9).

In view of God who punishes sin, His justice is an expression of divine wrath. This characteristic is seen in places like 2 Thessalonians 1:8, where it speaks of Jesus "taking vengeance on them that know not God, and that obey not the gospel of our Lord Jesus Christ." Louis Berkhof explains,

"The primary purpose of the punishment of sin is the maintenance of right and justice."[1]

The justice of God should evoke a sense of fear and dread for the lost and a sense of gratitude for the saved. As believers, we can take comfort that "God hath not appointed us to wrath, but to obtain salvation by our Lord Jesus Christ" (1 Thess. 5:9).

So how is a person counted "right" before God? You are counted righteous and "not guilty" before God by *believing* that Jesus lived a perfect life for you and died to pay the penalty for your sins. This transaction between the Christian and Christ was "to declare, I say, at this time [God's] righteousness: that he might be just, and the justifier of him which believeth in Jesus" (Rom. 3:26).

Righteousness is the earned merit of perfect obedience to God. We are neither perfect nor obedient, so we are not righteous. But Jesus perfectly obeyed all of the law of God *for us* who believe. Jesus has accomplished *for* us everything that God has required *of* us in the law. Consequently, as a believer, that perfect record of Christ is transferred to your account and God declares you to be "righteous" because you are united to His righteous Son. Paul writes, "For he hath made him to be sin for us, who knew no sin; that we might be made the righteousness of God in him" (2 Cor. 5:21). This transaction was both an expression of divine love and grace as well as an effectual means by which He satisfied His divine justice.

A final word needs to be said about God's justice in restoring the broken, the outcast, the poor, the orphan, and

---

1. Berkhof, *Systematic Theology*, 76.

the widow. God is in the business of looking after the outcast and the broken—keeping them as a central part in the so-called "mercy ministry" of His people. God's Word is full of exhortations and commands to seek mercy and justice for the oppressed. Consider a few of them:

He doth execute the judgment of the fatherless and widow, and loveth the stranger, in giving him food and raiment. (Deut. 10:18)

Learn to do well; seek judgment, relieve the oppressed, judge the fatherless, plead for the widow. (Isa. 1:17)

What doth the LORD require of thee, but to do justly, and to love mercy, and to walk humbly with thy God? (Mic. 6:8)

Woe unto you, scribes and Pharisees, hypocrites! for ye pay tithe of mint and anise and cummin, and have omitted the weightier matters of the law, judgment, mercy, and faith. (Matt. 23:23)

Pure religion and undefiled before God and the Father is this, To visit the fatherless and widows in their affliction, and to keep himself unspotted from the world. (James 1:27)

God's justice, then, is part of God's character. It is an expression of reward for righteousness and punishment for sin, and it is a desire to see equity among His people. May your meditation on the justice of God translate into a gospel-driven action for expressing His mercy and justice in the broken world around you.

REFLECTION QUESTIONS

1. As a just God, why does He require punishment for sin?

2. What part does justice play in the reconciliation of your relationship with God? What part does Jesus play in that reconciliation?

3. Why did Jesus have to be perfect and righteous to be our substitute on the cross?

4. Our passage in Deuteronomy 32 states that God is both faithful and just. How do these two attributes relate? What if God was just only *some* of the time? Why does He have to be both at the same time?

5. We were created in God's image (Gen. 1:27), which means, in part, that we are to reflect His character. How can you practically reflect God's justice in the world, especially to the poor, the outcast, the widow, and the orphan?

DIGGING DEEPER

- Some other Scripture passages on the justice of God include Deuteronomy 7:9–13; 2 Chronicles 6:15; Psalm 99:4; Isaiah 1:17; 3:10–11; Micah 6:8; 7:20; Matthew 25:41; Romans 1:32; 2:6; 6:23; 1 Corinthians 4:7; 2 Thessalonians 1:8; and 1 Peter 1:17.

- "Doing justice" for the outcast, the poor, and the broken is a matter of obedience, not just sympathy.

- Look up the definition of "propitiation" (cf. Rom. 3:25; 1 John 2:2). How might this relate to God's justice?

- See J. I. Packer, *Knowing God* (Downers Grove, Ill.: IVP Books, 1993).

29

GOD IS JEALOUS

SCRIPTURE MEDITATION

Thou shalt worship no other god: for the LORD, whose name is Jealous, is a jealous God.

—EXODUS 34:14

PRAYER

Heavenly Father, as I meditate on what the Bible says about Thy holy jealousy to glorify Thyself in the lives of Thy people, I ask for a humble and contrite heart. Move me from a man-centered way of thinking and feeling to a God-centered heart that considers my greatest joy and goal to be Thy glory. Help me to abandon all idols, to have no other gods before Thee. Thou knowest that which my heart must yield to Thee. Turn to me and be gracious to me. Lead me now in Thy truth, for Christ's sake. Amen.

BIBLICAL PERSPECTIVE

Whether we think of the jealousy of Rachel and Leah (Genesis 29–30) or of Joseph's brothers (Genesis 37), jealousy among humans can be a fiery passion of love or rage (Prov. 6:34; Song 8:6). But the God who is an infinite, eternal, and immutable Spirit cannot be swayed by passions like ours. Human jealousy is often destructive and rooted in sin (Job 5:2; Prov. 6:34; James 3:14, 16). There is, however, a righteous jealousy that burns for the glory of God's word and worship (Ps. 69:9; 119:139). We see this when Jesus Christ takes a whip and clears the temple (John 2:17). Thus, the words "be jealous" can also be understood to mean "be zealous" in a positive sense. God said, "I the LORD thy God am a jealous God" (Ex. 20:5; Deut. 5:9).

We can define God's jealousy as His limitless, fervent zeal to glorify Himself in the lives of His people. God's jealousy is the fervent energy of His holiness (Josh. 24:19). Impelled by His holiness, God's jealousy inflames both His wrath and His love into vigorous action. He says, "[I] will be jealous for my holy name" so that He will be "sanctified" in the sight of men and they will "know that I am the LORD" (Ezek. 39:25, 27–28).

Let's consider three word-pictures the Scriptures give us to express God's jealousy. First is the picture of *a husband zealous for his exclusive relationship with his wife*. Two of Ezekiel's parables depict Israel as God's adulterous wife who gives her love away to idols and mighty men—thus provoking God's jealousy and fury (Ezek. 16:38, 42; 23:25). The prophet's vivid images come directly from God's warning against worshiping other gods or any idols, because He is "jealous" and will not tolerate "whoring" after other gods (Ex. 20:5; 34:14–16). God's people are bound to Him by covenant; we must be exclusively His. No creature or image may intrude into that sacred relationship (Deut. 32:16, 21; Josh. 24:19–20). God has a zeal for His exclusive claim on your worship and supreme love.

The second picture of God's jealousy is *the fierceness of a warrior rushing into battle*. Isaiah 42:13 says, "The LORD shall go forth as a mighty man, he shall stir up jealousy like a man of war: he shall cry, yea, roar; he shall prevail against his enemies." God is the divine warrior who clothes Himself in righteousness, salvation, vengeance, and "zeal" (59:17). The military picture of jealousy shows us God's untiring zeal and the overwhelming motivation of His glorious divine nature to overcome His enemies.

In the third picture, God's jealousy is like *fire*, whether the fire of *love* (Song 8:6) or, more often, the fire of *anger* (Deut. 29:20; Ps. 79:5). The fire of jealousy is God's very being: "For the LORD thy God is a consuming fire, even a jealous God" (Deut. 4:24). This fire connects divine jealousy to a major biblical sign of God's presence: the pillar of fire or cloud of glory (Lev. 9:23–10:2; Neh. 9:12; Isa. 4:5; Mark 9:7). This picture of jealousy reveals the infinitely intense energy of God's affection as He dwells with His people.

God's jealousy often engages His wrath to punish sinners (Deut. 6:15; Josh. 24:19–20; Nah. 1:2). Though primarily directed at covenant breakers in Israel, God said the "fire of my jealousy" would devour all nations (Zeph. 3:8). However, divine jealousy also manifests itself in God's zeal for the salvation of His people (Isa. 59:17). "The zeal of the LORD of hosts" guarantees their deliverance and enjoyment of the everlasting kingdom (2 Kings 19:31; Isa. 9:7; 37:32). God has willed to exercise His jealousy for His holy name in the manifestation of His glory in Christ, with the destruction of His enemies and the redemption of a people who will return His zealous love for them with a love of all-consuming zeal (Titus 2:13–14).

The doctrine of divine jealousy teaches us that God's love and hatred are infinitely robust and intense. We should never consider God to be half-hearted in anything that He wills. His very essence is an eternal act of immeasurable love (1 John 4:8).

Let us consider from James 4 how God's jealousy ought to affect our Christian walk. First, we must *repent of ungodly desires and pursuits.* James points out a problem that can affect any church: "From whence come wars and fightings among you? come they not hence, even of your lusts that war in your members?" (v. 1). Churches and families have been destroyed by unchecked lusts and the sins that find fertile soil in them: infighting, covetousness, and friendship with the world (vv. 3–4). Then, driven by the intensity of God's holy, burning jealousy over His people, comes the charge, "ye adulterers and adulteresses" (v. 4). James then asks, "Or do you think that the Scripture says in vain, 'The Spirit who dwells in us yearns jealously'?" (v. 5, NKJV). This is a forceful wake-up call heated with God's holy jealousy that calls us to turn away from the heart-corruptions of worldliness and turn to God in love. The Spirit who yearns for our friendship with God will convict us of compromise.

Second, we must *pursue holiness and humility.* James gives a positive directive that is coupled with the call to repent from worldliness: "But he giveth more grace. Wherefore he saith, God resisteth the proud, but giveth grace unto the humble" (v. 6). When we realize the intensity of God's holy jealousy over our worship, our affections, our choices, and our commitment to His glory, we feel our need for a holiness that touches all of life. Let us in humility turn to God for the grace we need to pursue holiness and the love of

God more consistently and intentionally. A humble plea for grace is not passive, but active: we must submit to God, resist the devil, "draw nigh to God," cleanse our hands, be afflicted, mourn, and weep (vv. 7–8). The encouragement of a promise spurs us on: "Humble yourselves in the sight of the Lord, and he shall lift you up" (v. 10).

Third, we must *strive for unity with fellow believers*. In the context of James's wake-up call to humble repentance in view of God's jealousy, there are "wars and fightings among you" and believers "that speaketh evil of his brother, and judgeth his brother" (vv. 1, 11). God's burning jealously is kindled against us not only when we fail to love Him, but also when we mistreat and fail to love one another because of our worldly desires.

REFLECTION QUESTIONS

1. Consider some of the Scripture passages about destructive human jealousy rooted in rage and folly (Job 5:2; Prov. 6:34; 14:20; 24:1; James 3:14, 16). How is God's jealousy different in its source, motives, manner, and goals?

2. How does God's jealousy help us to differentiate righteous human jealousy from unrighteous human jealousy?

3. Think of how the Spirit yearns for our friendship with God and convicts us of compromise: "Or do you think that the Scripture says in vain, 'The Spirit who dwells in us yearns jealously'?" (James 4:5 NKJV). What things, habits, or people in your life hinder your friendship with God?

4. How does God's holy jealousy relate to our need to humble ourselves and pursue holiness?

5. How does God's holy jealousy relate to our call to love fellow believers and live in unity with one another?

DIGGING DEEPER

- Some other Scripture passages on the jealousy of God include Exodus 9:16; Deuteronomy 4:23–25; 6:14–15; 29:18–20; 32:16, 21–22; 1 Kings 14:22–23; Psalms 78:58; 79:5; Ezekiel 8:3, 5; 20:14; 23:25; 36:5; 38:19; Joel 2:18; Zephaniah 1:18; 3:8; Zechariah 1:14–16; 1 Corinthians 10:21–22; 2 Corinthians 11:2; and Hebrews 10:27.

- Erik Thoennes says, "The prevalence of a consumer mentality and human-centeredness in contemporary society easily leads our agendas and takes greater priority than God's glory. A desire to be relevant and attractive can encourage a marketing mentality in the church that lacks jealousy for God's honor. The heavy influence of secular psychology, with its therapeutic, self-centered approach to ministry, also can detract from God's glory being the supreme objective when Christians gather. These influences can lead the church to become a pragmatically oriented self-help group rather than a God-glorifying community. On the other hand, when God's people deeply desire that he be glorified so that nothing competes with him for our devotion and worship, they should experience a godly jealousy that mirrors his." In the reforms of Hezekiah, Jehoiada, and Josiah, "jealousy on behalf of God's name, and his exclusive right to receive worship and covenant fidelity, was a primary motivating emotion."[1]

- See also K. Erik Thoennes, *Godly Jealousy: A Theology of Intolerant Love* (Fearn, Ross-shire, Scotland: Christian Focus, 2005).

---

1. Erik Thoennes, "Redeeming Jealousy: The Glory of God's Exclusive Love," Desiring God, July 15, 2019, accessed February 6, 2020, https://www.desiringgod.org/articles/redeeming-jealousy.

30

GOD IS COMPASSIONATE

SCRIPTURE MEDITATION

In all their affliction he was afflicted, and the angel of his presence saved them: in his love and in his pity he redeemed them; and he bare them, and carried them all the days of old.
—ISAIAH 63:9

PRAYER

Gracious and longsuffering Jehovah, I worship Thee because of Thy tender compassion toward me, for Thou hast regarded my misery in sin, sent Thy Son to accomplish my salvation, and sent Thy Spirit to bring the power of the gospel to my heart. Thy merciful compassion adorns all of sacred history. Let Thy compassion always be my object lesson, that I may imitate Thee in how I treat the sin-stricken and miserable. Be Thou mighty in compassion to save. I pray this in Jesus's name. Amen.

BIBLICAL PERSPECTIVE

Our meditation on God's compassion takes us to the book of Exodus, where the story of God's rescue of His people begins with their cry of affliction in Egyptian bondage. One of the first actions God takes emphasizes His compassion: "God heard their groaning, and God remembered his covenant…. And God looked upon the children of Israel, and God had respect unto them" (Ex. 2:24–25). When God said, "I have surely seen the affliction of my people," He added, "for I know their sorrows; and I am come down to deliver them" (Ex. 3:7–8). Centuries later, the exiles returning from Babylon called upon this God who hears, sees, and acknowledges His people's affliction, addressing Him as the One who "didst see the affliction of our fathers in Egypt, and heardest their cry by the Red sea" (Neh. 9:9). Likewise, the psalmist remembered that, even though His people provoked Him many times, "Nevertheless he regarded their affliction, when he heard their cry" (Ps. 106:44). Behold God's unspeakable compassion!

How is it that God's compassion reaches the misery of His people's affliction so deeply? Isaiah remarkably explains that "in all their affliction he was afflicted…in his love and in his pity he redeemed them; and he bare them, and carried them all the days of old" (Isa. 63:9). It is striking that God, in compassion for His people, counted their oppression in Egypt as His own. This does not mean that God suffers sorrow, but rather, as Isaiah wrote, that God has "love" and "pity" for His suffering people that moves Him to rescue them. His sensitivity to their sorrow is expressed in terms of deep inner feelings (v. 15): "bowels" and "mercies."

The compassionate heart of God drives the progress of salvation history. Over and over, God's goodness manifests itself in His mercy to the miserable. God is aware of His people's suffering with a compassion that engages Him to support and deliver them.

God's compassionate heart delights to save repentant sinners. When the children of Israel saw that they had sinned against their God by serving the gods of the nations, they put away these "strange gods" and cried to the Lord for deliverance. The Lord saw the distress of His chastened people, and "his soul was grieved for the misery of Israel" (Judg. 10:16). The expression "his soul" is a bold anthropomorphism (a metaphor using human terms for God) that communicates God's eager willingness to rescue the repentant. God delights to welcome and bless those who turn back to Him (Luke 15:20).

God's compassion reaches out to His elect people before they turn to Him. The holy God will not violate His covenant, but will save His people despite their sins. God's compassion reflects not a volatile or fickle temperament that changes from one mood to another, but His faithfulness and steady love for His elect.

As it impacts our lives, God's compassion calls us to worship Him, to seek Him in all our afflictions, to be compassionate toward others, and to carefully meditate on salvation history. First, *God's compassion engenders worship*. When the people knew that God "had looked upon their affliction" and had visited them to deliver them, "they bowed their heads and worshipped" (Ex. 4:31). We too must continually recall the misery in which sin plunged us and how Christ responded to our misery by putting Himself forth as a propitiation to free us from our sins. Let us worship Him with hearts full of gratitude.

Second, God's compassion should draw us like a magnet *to seek Him in all our troubles and sorrows*. God is not distant and aloof from His children, but is full of kindness and sensitive affection toward us. Psalm 34:17–18 says, "The righteous cry, and the LORD heareth, and delivereth them out of all their troubles. The LORD is nigh unto them that are of a broken heart; and saveth such as be of a contrite spirit." When it seems that trials come like waves, one after another, remind yourself of this precious promise: "Humble yourselves therefore under the mighty hand of God, that he may exalt you in due time: casting all your care upon him; for he careth for you" (1 Peter 5:6–7).

Third, we must *imitate the compassion God has for sinners by showing compassion to the weak and miserable*. This describes all of us, for in one way or another all of God's covenant people have been shown compassion in their weakness and misery. We must therefore "be ye kind one to another, tenderhearted, forgiving one another, even as God for Christ's sake hath forgiven you" (Eph. 4:32).

Fourth, God's compassion calls us *to be careful students of Scripture*, especially when we meet with trials. Let us be those who can always trace the compassion of God revealed in salvation history and apply it to our situation. From God's gracious response to the cry of the afflicted Israelites, through the manger and cross of Christ who was sent to save the miserable, to the right hand of the throne of God where our risen High Priest ever intercedes for us (Heb. 4:14–16)—may our hearts and minds resound more loudly with the history of God's saving compassion than the noise of the disappointments that cross our paths.

REFLECTION QUESTIONS

1. Take some time to meditate about and record several specific ways God has shown you compassion in recent years.

2. Think of the striking compassion of God in salvation history that "in all their affliction he was afflicted" (Isa. 63:9). How does this magnify God's compassion in your current situation?

3. Why is it essential that God is both moved by compassion for His people and yet unchangeable?

4. Consider Christ's compassion as both His willingness and ability to sympathize with us. The same body once pierced by the nails and the same heart once broken by betrayal are now at the right hand of God, obtaining grace for all who draw near to God through Him. Christ knows, Christ understands, and Christ is able to help. How does this truth affect you?

5. Which of the applications above is most critical to your current situation? What application would you add that is not included in this chapter?

DIGGING DEEPER

• Some other Scripture passages about God's compassion include Psalms 78:38–39; 86:15; 103:13; Lamentations 3:22–23; Micah 7:19; Matthew 9:36; 14:14; Mark 6:34; Luke 15:20; 2 Corinthians 1:2–4; and Colossians 3:12.

• God's compassion does not require divine suffering. The cross of Christ does not reveal divine suffering, but the fulfillment of God's will (Isa. 53:10–11; Col. 1:19–20). In Acts 9:4, when Christ says, "Saul, why persecutest thou me?", He is not making a plea as divine sufferer, but making a summons as sovereign Lord. The thrust of divine compassion is not divine pain, but divine power to save and judge. Therefore, we must disagree with Dietrich Bonhoeffer (1906–1945), who said, "Only the suffering God can help."[1] Yet we must be careful not to overcorrect and deny the compassion of God. We declare God's immutability for His glory and man's good. God does not ride a roller coaster of emotions and pain with His people, and yet God's people can find in the unchanging One constant strength, steadiness, stability, and a special affection for them in their sorrows. God fully relates to

---

1. Dietrich Bonhoeffer, *Works, Volume 8, Letters and Papers from Prison* (Minneapolis: Fortress, 2009), 479.

His creatures with love and mercy, yet without divine distress or change.[2]

- See also Joshua Mack, *Compassion: Seeing with Jesus' Eyes* (Phillipsburg, N.J.: P&R, 2015); Rob Lister, *God is Impassible and Impassioned: Toward a Theology of Divine Emotion* (Wheaton, Ill.: Crossway, 2013); Thomas G. Weinandy, *Does God Suffer?* (Notre Dame, Ind.: University of Notre Dame Press, 2000).

---

2. Thomas G. Weinandy, *Does God Suffer?* (Notre Dame, Ind.: University of Notre Dame Press, 2000), 165.

31 GOD IS GLORIOUS

SCRIPTURE MEDITATION

For God, who commanded the light to shine out of darkness, hath shined in our hearts, to give the light of the knowledge of the glory of God in the face of Jesus Christ. But we have this treasure in earthen vessels, that the excellency of the power may be of God, and not of us.

—2 CORINTHIANS 4:6–7

PRAYER

Glorious God, Thou art of supreme value and worth. Thou art glorious in Thy manifold character. Thou art the greatest Treasure in the universe and, by Thy grace, Thou hast become *my* Treasure. I am but a clay pot, easily broken and weak. And yet, Thou hast placed within me the glories of Thyself and of Thy gospel to show that the surpassing power belongs to Thee. As I meditate upon Thy glory, fill me with awe and wonder about Thee at Thy throne of grace. I pray this in Christ's name. Amen.

BIBLICAL PERSPECTIVE

God's glory refers specifically to His divine essence and ultimate greatness. It is the display of the sum total of God's manifold perfections. As the sun shines beams of light, so God's character shines beams of glory. The apostle John explains, "I saw no temple therein: for the Lord God Almighty and the Lamb are the temple of it. And the city had no need of the sun, neither of the moon, to shine in it: for the glory of God did lighten it, and the Lamb is the light thereof" (Rev. 21:22–23). God's glory, then, is the expression of His essential nature, which is also represented by His honor and His name.

Throughout the Bible, God repeatedly refers to His sovereign works, His revelation, and His covenant promises in relation to His *name*. Consider a few of these passages as they relate His glory to His name:

> Give unto the LORD the glory due unto his name; worship the LORD in the beauty of holiness. (Ps. 29:2)

> Make a joyful noise unto God, all ye lands: sing forth the honour of his name: make his praise glorious. (Ps. 66:1–2)

> Help us, O God of our salvation, for the glory of thy name: and deliver us, and purge away our sins, for thy name's sake. (Ps. 79:9)

His name is like a directional marker—pointing to His character, promises, and mighty works. In other words, when we say that we "praise His name," we are saying that we praise His glorious attributes as they exist in His nature and as they are expressed throughout His creation.

In fact, creation itself bears witness to the glory of God: "The heavens declare the glory of God; and the firmament sheweth his handywork" (Ps. 19:1). As Isaiah is taken aback by His vision of the Lord, he tells of the proclamation of the seraphim: "Holy, holy, holy, is the LORD of hosts: the whole earth is full of his glory" (Isa. 6:3). Creation, then, also points—like a directional arrow—to God's perfect character and attributes.

Similarly, the Bible speaks of "giving glory" to God or "glorifying" Him: "Let them give glory unto the LORD, and declare his praise" (Isa. 42:12). In this sense, giving glory to God means praising Him for His worth, His character, and simply for who He is. In fact, in everything we do, we should seek to give Him glory and praise. As Paul writes, "Whether therefore ye eat, or drink, or whatsoever ye do, do all to the glory of God" (1 Cor. 10:31). When we "give" glory to God, we are not literally giving Him something as if He lacked a part of holiness or essential greatness. Rather, we are acknowledging and ascribing praise *because* of His greatness and perfect character. Glory and praise, as our response to the expression of His character, are synonymous (Phil. 1:11). When we "glorify" His name (cf. Ps. 86:9; Luke 2:20), we are praising Him and lifting Him up as the only true and living God.

The *greatest* expression, however, of God's glory is in the incarnation (God becoming man) of His eternal Son, Jesus Christ. In Jesus, we find the full display of God's manifold character. Jesus has taken sinners, who have fallen short of the glory of God (Rom. 3:23), and has become their "hope of glory" (Col. 1:27). In other words, Jesus—for whom "it pleased the Father that in him should all fulness dwell"

(Col. 1:19)—has set up residence in our hearts by His Spirit (Gal. 4:6). He now grants us access not only to come directly before God's throne of grace (Heb. 4:16), but also to enter glory itself—our heavenly home (Col. 3:4).

The apostle Paul writes, "But we all, with open face beholding as in a glass the glory of the Lord, are changed into the same image from glory to glory" (2 Cor. 3:18). Likewise, he explains, Jesus Himself "shall change our vile body, that it may be fashioned like unto his glorious body" (Phil. 3:21). As pilgrims, we make our way through this troubled life, looking unto the Author and Finisher of our faith (Heb. 12:2), until we are *glorified* in the presence of God (Rom. 8:30).

REFLECTION QUESTIONS

1. What do you think "darkness" refers to in 2 Corinthians 4:6? What part of humanity does Paul relate darkness to? Read Luke 11:34–36; John 3:19; Romans 1:21; and Ephesians 4:18. What do these say about the nature of "darkness"?

2. What is the "light" in 2 Corinthians 4:6?

3. How do we *get* the light of the knowledge of the glory of God in the face of Jesus Christ?

4. God gives us the "knowledge" of what?

5. If God's glory is the display of His attributes and character, then how is His glory seen "in the face of Jesus Christ"? More specifically (and a little deeper), how are God's love *and* holiness seen in the person and work of Jesus?

6. In 2 Corinthians 4:7, Paul refers to the gospel as "this treasure in earthen vessels" or jars of clay. What images come to your mind when you think about a jar of clay or a clay pot? What is the reasoning that Paul gives in verse 7 for equating jars of clay with broken, sinful believers?

7. Read verse 7 again and then read 2 Corinthians 12:9. Why should we "boast" of our weaknesses?

DIGGING DEEPER

- Some other Scripture passages on the glory of God include Exodus 24:16; 1 Chronicles 16:24; Psalms 19:1; 24:7; 86:12; 96:3; 145:5; Isaiah 4:2; 6:3; 48:11; Luke 2:14; John 1:14; 13:31; 17:1; Ephesians 3:16; Philippians 3:21; Colossians 3:4; 2 Thessalonians 1:10; 1 Peter 4:11; and Revelation 21:23.

- One of the battle cries of the Protestant Reformation was *soli Deo gloria*, "to God alone be the glory!" The Reformers wanted to see a fundamental shift in theology, worship, and church government from a focus on man to a focus on God. All of life is to be for the glory of God alone—not man.

- Paul writes in Romans 1:23, that sinful man "changed the glory of the uncorruptible God into an image made like to corruptible man." How would a person exchange God's glory for idols?

- See also Christopher W. Morgan and Robert A. Peterson, eds., *The Glory of God* (Wheaton, Ill.: Crossway, 2010); John Piper, *God's Passion for His Glory: Living the Vision of Jonathan Edwards* (Wheaton, Ill.: Crossway, 1998).

TRUTHFORLIFE®

THE BIBLE-TEACHING MINISTRY OF **ALISTAIR BEGG**

The mission of Truth For Life is to teach the Bible with clarity and relevance so that unbelievers will be converted, believers will be established, and local churches will be strengthened.

Daily Program

Each day, Truth For Life distributes the Bible teaching of Alistair Begg across the U.S. and in several locations outside of the U.S. through 1,800 radio outlets. To find a radio station near you, visit **truthforlife.org/stationfinder**.

Free Teaching

The daily program, and Truth For Life's entire teaching archive of over 2,000 Bible-teaching messages, can be accessed for free online and through Truth For Life's full-feature mobile app. Download the free mobile app at **truthforlife.org/app** and listen free online at **truthforlife.org**.

At-Cost Resources

Books and full-length teaching from Alistair Begg on CD, DVD, and USB are available for purchase at cost, with no markup. Visit **truthforlife.org/store**.

Where to Begin?

If you're new to Truth For Life and would like to know where to begin listening and learning, find starting point suggestions at **truthforlife. org/firststep**. For a full list of ways to connect with Truth For Life, visit **truthforlife.org/subscribe**.

Contact Truth For Life

P.O. Box 398000 Cleveland, Ohio 44139
phone 1 (888) 588-7884   **email** letters@truthforlife.org
 /truthforlife   @truthforlife   truthforlife.org